Ned Halley is the wine columnist for *Ideal Home*, and has contributed to a number of specialist magazines, including *Decanter* and *Wine*. He is a member of the Wine Writers' Circle.

A freelance writer for the last five years, he began as a reporter with the *Hongkong Standard*. Subsequent jobs took him to the diverse domains of *Mayfair* and *Reader's Digest*.

Ned Halley lives with his wife and two children in Somerset.

GW00708155

The Cheap Wine Guide

Ned Halley

SPHERE BOOKS LIMITED

For Mama

Contents

Author's Note

Why a *cheap* wine guide? The answer is simple: I believe that, to date, there have been two kinds of wine; one is the kind that people drink and the other is the kind that gets written about.

The more expensive a wine is, the more profit it makes for the producer, the middlemen, the retailer, even the tax people. So the wine trade enthusiastically promotes its more expensive lines by inviting bibulous hacks like me to lavish tastings – and even to visit the vineyards in far-flung parts where the raw materials come from.

So, the wines that get written about tend to be the posher ones with a bit of a story behind them – and a good margin for the trade. Fair enough. But what about the other kind, the supermarket 'plonks' at the distant and untrumpeted end of the price scale?

The answer is that everybody drinks them – including all but the very snootiest of the wine writers of my acquaintance – but nobody expects to read about them in the solemn tomes of vinous esoterica that we call wine books. I read a lot of wine books, rather in the way that armchair horticulturists read gardening books (for sheer amazement-value – the gardens, or the wine prices in my case, being so utterly unattainable) and have lately discovered that virtually none of the wines we drink at home ever seem to get a mention.

Hence the *Cheap Wine Guide*, which starts with the premiss that all the wines mentioned in it must be cheap, and must be available in the high street, or at least by mail order. I have researched this book by buying the wines I wanted to write about, and drinking them at home. On a number of occasions, I have had tasting sessions in which a number of selfless and courageous cronies have sipped (and in many cases gagged over) a dozen or two choice plonks. And I have come up with several hundred cheap wines that I can recommend as good value for money.

To a great extent, this book is a guide to where the cheap wines are, rather than a qualitative assessment of the lower rungs in the wine-price ladder. But some cheap wines are, I believe, remarkable value for money, so I have used a simple star-rating formula to highlight those better buys. (See the listings starting on page 23.)

I have tried to explain in the most basic terms what each type of wine tastes like, and a little bit about its background. I have done this because I believe it really does make a wine more interesting if you know something about it – and if I didn't believe that wine was a genuinely fascinating topic, I wouldn't write about it.

Finally, a couple of thank-yous. One to the many retailers who have co-operated so helpfully in supplying last-minute price and vintage details of the wines (sadly, quite a number of good buys were discontinued or priced out of range between the time of writing and of going to press, and had to be deleted). And another thank-you to Helen Oliver, who masterminded the final correction of proofs in a heroic endeavour to make this book as accurate and up-to-date as humanly possible.

Introduction

The cheap wine on sale in Britain today is by no means nasty. There are, naturally, a few gruesome exceptions to the rule, but it certainly holds true that the least expensive wines available in this country are of a far higher quality than the cheapest of the wines consumed by our continental cousins.

Of course, everyday *vin explosif* or *vino collapso* costs less than Coke in France, Italy or Spain, where it can be bought draught from the barrel and free of tax. Convert the local price into sterling, and it may well be under 50p a bottle. But there's a catch: the wine tastes coarse, raw, mouth-puckering. It's not the sort of stuff we Brits like to drink at home.

What's more, that 50p bottle of the roughest plonk would be very poor value if bought from a shop in Britain. That is because once duty and VAT are added, the price becomes £1.40; and once the cost of transport and the trade's mark-ups are piled on top of that, the wine reaches £2.00 – or rather £1.99 when the bottle finally finds its way on to the off-licence shelf.

The £2 Miracle

Happily, for the same price as that bottle of rough plonk there are a host of delicious wines to be found. This is primarily because the British grocery trade has taken it into its head to flog vast quantities of good, everyday wine just as it sells similarly huge amounts of good, everyday food, soap suds and other necessities.

Currently the world's most important market for the international wine trade, Britain has the biggest choice of different wines available anywhere. Winemakers fall over themselves to get into our market – which has quadrupled since 1970 – offering their wares at prices they know they must keep to a minimum because of the punitive duty and tax that will be added before the product reaches the public.

Because the volume of wine sales has grown so rapidly, the trade has been able to keep its margins in check, and yet maintain healthy profits. This has meant, too, that the important £2.00 threshold for cheap wines has been maintained. Indeed, there are far more good, inexpensive wines on the market now than there were five years ago – in spite of more than 50 per cent general price inflation and a 10 per cent rise in duty in the mean time.

Quality has simultaneously improved, partly because buyers have successfully sought out new sources – particularly in the Mediterranean countries – and partly owing to new winemaking technology, which has helped growers overcome every kind of production problem, from worms to weather.

Prices at the lower end of the scale have also remained stable because there is, quite simply, far too much wine chasing too few drinkers. Consumption in the two thirstiest countries, France and Italy, has plummeted in recent years, and yet production has been boosted. The EEC wine lake has consequently reached a mind-boggling figure, something like 2 billion bottles – or three times the amount drunk in Britain every year.

This veritable ocean of unwanted wine, created by crackpot Common Market agricultural policies which guarantee growers an income even if they cannot sell what they produce, consists entirely of low-grade plonk only fit for conversion into industrial alcohol. But the very existence of such excess over demand is sufficient to persuade those who make wine of better quality that the market is very definitely a buyer's one.

Thus, wine under £2 a bottle continues to proliferate. And if your budget stretches as far as £3, there are some marvellous bottles to be had. Cheap-wine *cognoscenti* know, indeed, that the £3 bottle is substantially better value than the £2 one because the value of the wine itself is a very much greater part of the purchase price.

To explain: bottling, duty and transport are fixed costs regardless of the quality of wine in the bottle. Only the VAT at 15 per cent and the trade's mark-up at 20 to 25 per cent rise with the value of the contents. So the cost breakdowns of the £2 bottle and the £3 bottle look like this:

£2 bottle	£3 bottle
Duty 73p	Duty 73p
Transport 30p	Transport 30p
Mark-up 40p	Mark-up 60p
VAT 26p	VAT 40p
WINE 31p	WINE 97p

The moral of this story is that if you pay 50 per cent more, you get wine worth 300 per cent more. This happy formula does not, however, extend indefinitely up the price scale. A £4.50 bottle, for example, at 50 per cent more than the £3 one, has £1's worth more wine – a comparatively paltry improvement of 100 per cent.

King's New Clothes

You can prove anything with statistics, of course, but what really counts about wine is whether it is good to drink – whatever the price. And the trouble with expensive wines is that they tend to raise the drinker's expectations of how good the wine should taste, without in any way guaranteeing that it will be the least bit more delicious than another wine costing half as much.

Price, in other words, is no indicator of how much you are going to like a wine. My own belief is that to enjoy a really expensive wine to the full, you have to *know* it is a greatly reputed little number and therefore be primed to expect what the hype merchants would call a 'taste experience'. So if your interest in wine extends only as far as how good it tastes, and you could not care less whether it comes from a south-facing slope or a vineyard with medieval origins, you are likely to find expensive, cult wines very poor value for money.

I have personally tried numerous wines with astronomical price tags and found them frankly disappointing. But when tasting among colleagues from the wine-writing fraternity, I must admit to a faint heart when it comes to playing the *ingénu* (wine-writer's code-word for a complete ignoramus), and I have yet to take a gulp of £200-a-bottle Château this-or-that and then proclaim that I prefer Sainsbury's own-label at £1.99.

At 'blind' tastings where the wines are assessed without their names or prices being revealed to the tasters, cheap wines have often confounded me by leaving pricey ones in the shade quality-wise. And I am not alone; the specialist wine magazines are always full of blind-tasting reports where the supermarket plonks have been pointedly preferred to renowned and ruinously costly brands.

None of this need overly concern the cheap-wine buff, but it is at least comforting to know that if your absolute maximum budget for any bottle of wine is £3, you really won't be missing all that much.

Bottle Sizes

There is no universal standard, yet, for the sizes of wine bottles, but virtually all the wines sold in Britain come in either 70cl (1.23 pints), 75cl (1.32 pints) or 1 litre (1.76 pints) sizes. 'Party-size' bottles may be magnum size – 1.5 litres (2.64 pints), or even bigger.

As a *very* general rule, cheaper wines come in 70cl bottles. Supermarket own-label bottles, for example, have long been this size. From 1 January 1989, all wines from EEC countries will have to be in standardized 75cl bottles, and some retailers are already moving up to this size with their own-brands. Sainsbury's, for example, have by now changed all their wines to 75cl bottles. On the whole, smart wines from individual estates come in 75cl bottles (though many grand German makers stick parsimoniously to the 70cl size).

It's all very confusing, and has served the wine trade well when it has been striving to maintain sub-£2 prices for basic plonks. On a pro rata basis, after all, a 70cl bottle priced at £1.99 would cost £2.13 at 75cl. Litre prices can be misleading too: bear in mind when you're bargain-hunting that the litre price equivalent to the £1.99 70cl bottle is £2.84.

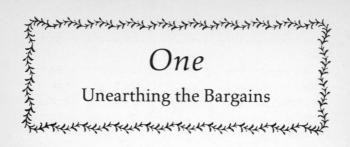

One

Unearthing the Bargains

As commodities go, wine must be one of the most erratically priced of all. Identical brands are offered at prices which can vary quite breathtakingly, for wines at both ends of the price spectrum. So, shop around for bargains.

The catch is that no one retailer – or wholesaler – is consistently cheaper than all others. Certain outlets undercut the opposition in wines from particular countries, while some shops prefer to do a special line in very cheap wines from anywhere. This admirable latter policy is particularly true of two supermarket giants, Sainsbury's and Tesco, which have for some years maintained a remarkable stock of wines under £2 – many of them very good indeed. Another supermarket chain, Waitrose – which has branches throughout most of the southern half of England – lives by the 'Never Knowingly Undersold' maxim of the John Lewis Partnership of which it is part. This also means some real bargains for those fortunate enough to have a branch to hand, although it cannot be said that Waitrose makes a big speciality of very cheap wines.

Much of the rock-bottom wine is of the 'own-label' variety, and a chain offering good basic plonks under its own livery is Asda, the 100-branch supermarket arm of Associated Dairies. With about fifty own-label wines around or under £2.50, Asda is fast becoming a strong contender with the likes of Tesco – for quality as well as value.

The biggest wine retailer, in terms of number of outlets, is the Co-op. About 2,300 of its 3,300 shops and supermarkets are licensed, and many sell a respectable range of cheap wines. Co-op 'superstores' have the largest choice on offer, but there is no guarantee that any particular wine will be stocked in a given branch, as the decision about what to sell or not to sell is taken on a local rather than a national basis. All very democratic, no doubt, but none too helpful to bargain-hunters in search of a recommended wine.

The Chain Gang

Supermarkets have now grabbed more than half of the take-home wine trade, leaving the traditional merchants to fight it out with each other for their ever-shrinking share of the market. It seems that the high-street chains have survived only because the overall wine market has increased so dramatically – we Brits drink four times as much wine in 1987 as we did in 1970 – and because there remains a strong traditional-minded group of shoppers who disdain the idea of buying their wine in an emporium as brassy as your average supermarket.

So high-street off-licences such as Victoria Wine, Thresher and Peter Dominic like to promote themselves as friendly neighbourhood wine merchants where personal service counts for a lot. Trouble is, few of these chain retailers employ shop managers who know much, if anything, about wine, so the 'personal service' element only extends as far as the fact that you pay the person behind the counter rather than some cash-register drone at the check-out.

Don't get too excited about the prospect of finding cheap wines in the chains. With many hundreds of branches to stock, buyers can rarely do 'bin-ends' (last of stock) sales at cut price and there are still very few good own-label plonks – though Victoria Wine have lately proved an honourable exception to this.

All the biggest chains are owned by brewing conglomerates, whose complex interests elsewhere in the drinks field significantly affect the sort of wines they stock. That's why, for example, Victoria Wine outlets are full of Grants of St James's branded wines – because both the shops and the brand are owned by Allied Breweries, whose other alcoholic concerns include such firms as Harveys of Bristol and Showerings (of Babycham renown).

Similarly, the Peter Dominic chain will be found to stock the well-known Piat wines and a range of smart Bordeaux wines from Gilbey of the Château de Loudenne. Both these French firms are owned by Dominic's proprietor, IDV, itself a subsidiary, along with Watneys, of the huge Grand Metropolitan group.

And so on. The upshot is that the chains are not exclusively guided by what their customers want, but at least partially by what their corporate partners wish to sell. The independence of the supermarket chains (well, most of them, anyway), on the other hand, leaves them free to buy in entirely what they like at what price they can negotiate – and when you are as big as Sainsbury's or Tesco, you have plenty of negotiating muscle.

So just what is there in favour of the high-street wine merchants when it comes to the quest for cheap wines? One unquestionable merit they have is that of convenience: you don't want to make a special trip to an out-of-town hypermarket to buy a £1.99 bottle of plonk, after all. And the merchants do have *some* bargains – see the listings which start on page 23.

If you are willing to buy a dozen or more bottles of wine at one time, most high-street merchants should offer you a discount – though this is unlikely to be more than 5 per cent. Some chains clearly advertise their discounts, at others you should ask. The reduction should apply to mixed dozens as well as to whole cases of the same wine.

Doing It Wholesale

Anyone prepared to fork out enough money to buy a dozen or more bottles certainly deserves a good deal from the wine merchant, and all kinds of firms do offer special 'wholesale' terms. Some merchants, in fact, are purely wholesale operations permitted to sell wine only in quantities of a dozen or more. (To sell retail – which means less than a case to any one customer – a retail licence is required.)

The anomalous licensing laws allow wholesale-only traders to operate more or less whenever they like. Thus, while on Sundays in England except between 12 noon and 2pm and between 7 and 10pm no retailers can sell alcohol, wholesalers can do a roaring trade in the stuff all day long.

What's more, the wholesale 'warehouses' that started springing up in the mid-1980s have been able to operate on very competitive margins – not needing the elaborate shopfitting and other pricey overheads that their retail rivals seem to require. Consequently, some warehouse prices are very low indeed, undercutting even the major supermarkets on branded wines.

Easily the leading warehouse firm is Majestic, which is expanding its outlet network at a remarkable pace. And for sheer volume of different varieties, it must be the number one seller of cheap wines: maybe 100 at under £2 (though not available in every outlet) and hundreds more under £3.

The brash style of the warehouses, however, is only one side of the wholesale wine business. The other, much more discreet, side is that part of the trade which supplies the independent retailers, the restaurants and wine bars, the catering industry as a whole. And there is no reason why such wholesalers should not supply the public, too, if the public can just track them down, brandishing its cash and showing a willingness to buy by the case.

Naturally, wholesalers wish to protect the interests of their clients in the catering industry by keeping their trade prices quiet. Accordingly, some wholesalers issue two separate lists – one for private customers, another for the trade. Other firms are more brazen, showing the two different lots of prices in the same list. As a rule, the gap between the two is around 20 per cent – certainly a saving worth having, and worth buying the wine in quantity to get.

Mail Order

Many wholesalers and specialist wine merchants (such as those who concentrate on wines from particular regions) offer a mail-order service. If you order enough wine, delivery is almost always free. You choose your wines from a list, which may be published either once or twice a year, and which includes all the information you need about payments, discounts and deliveries.

Mail-order merchants, it must be said, do not offer a vast number of cheap wines; posh Bordeaux and Burgundy are more commonly the speciality of the well-established London firms such as Berry Bros & Rudd, Corney & Barrow and Justerini & Brooks. But such merchants do sometimes offer remarkable value through their 'house' wines, and given that these are delivered to you, probably free of charge and at a discount if you order in any quantity, the wine can start to look like a bargain.

Some of the mail-order lists are in themselves a bit of a treat. Lay & Wheeler, of Colchester, offer more than 1,000 different wines from the pages of their glossy magazine-sized catalogue, which includes copious notes on individual bottles, with advice on when they will be at their best to drink.

On a similar scale is the list of the Suffolk merchants and brewers, Adnams. This vast catalogue is particularly entertaining, as it incorporates an often-hilarious running commentary from Adnams's eccentric wine director. Another attraction of the list which is perhaps more important is that it is issued only once a year, usually not too long after the Budget. Adnams's prices therefore do not increase until the following year – which can mean some good bargains if sterling is in one of its perennial slides against the currencies of the wine-growing countries.

Adnams, sadly, is one of the very few once-a-year lists, and nearly all merchants – supermarkets included – are forever easing their prices upwards in the hopes of making us pay more for the same wine. When inflation is low, merchants like to blame the poor old Pound for price rises; unhappily, there has never been much evidence of wine prices falling when sterling is on the up!

Buying Abroad

Day trips to Boulogne and Calais in the Volvo Estate to load up with gastronomic goodies may be a great giggle, but it means buying an awful lot of wine before the travelling expenses can be justified by the savings against UK prices.

Duty-wise, the whole thing works like this: HM Customs will graciously allow UK residents returning from abroad to bring 2 litres of duty-free still wine with them. Travellers who forgo the additional allowance of a bottle of spirits can instead bring a further 2 litres of duty-free wine. This applies to any still wine of 20 degrees alcohol or less.

For duty-*paid* wine – bought, say, in the supermarket rather than in the duty-free shop – the allowance is a rather more generous 8 litres per adult. That's a fraction short of a case of 70cl bottles each. But this applies to EEC countries only. Tourists returning from Bulgaria clutching a crate of best red will discover to their chagrin that their allowance is a mere 4 litres.

Amateur importers determined to pack in as much plonk as possible can expect to pay somewhat dearly for the privilege. In quantities above the aforementioned allowances, all wine is dutiable as follows:

EEC countries, per litre – £1.12
Non-EEC countries, per litre – £1.24

On top of the duty, Customs will also charge 15 per cent VAT on the purchase price of the wine – so travellers are expected to have a receipt. The upshot is that if you have, say, a dozen litres above your non-dutiable allowance of the roughest French wine bought for 5 francs (about 50p) a bottle, you will end up paying the Customs more than £14 in duty and tax. Each litre will consequently have cost a total of £1.70, compared to a likely price in Britain of not much more than £2 – assuming that you could find really *ordinaire* wine of a similarly humble pedigree on sale here, that is.

The only kind of wine that is worth importing from France in this way is the cheap stuff, because fine wines in France commonly cost *more* there than they do in Britain. Such is the rapacious nature of the French retailer that bargain bottles of the *grands vins* are less than abundant. Better buys are likely to be found at the vineyards themselves, where growers have taken more and more to selling wine at the farm gate, so to speak. Large co-operatives – where growers from the surrounding district bring their grapes to be incorporated into a blended range of wines – often have sales offices where the public are welcome to buy a case or two. (But remember, a receipt is needed for dutiable wines so the Customs can charge their VAT at the right figure.)

And what about taking a chance and trying to smuggle a crate or two in? When you bear in mind that the saving in duty is unlikely, even on expensive wine, to be more than £20 or so per case, the risk of detection doesn't look worth it. The penalties are positively Draconian. If you are caught with undeclared, dutiable grog, the whole lot is automatically forfeit – including the amount allowed duty-free. The smuggler must also pay all the duty, plus a bit added on as a penalty. And if the Customs officers are feeling out of sorts on that particular day, they may just take it into their heads to prosecute you for the crime of smuggling into the bargain.

At the Auctions

In 1986-7, prices fetched at auction for fine wines – the £50-a-bottle variety – have been falling, so rumours abound that there are all sorts of bargains to be had at Christie's, Sotheby's and so on. Unfortunately, prices for the cheapest wines have not shown a similar decline; in fact, buying plonk at auction has become a progressively costlier business with the introduction of buyers' premiums – usually about 10 per cent added on to the amount you think you have bought the wine for.

Provincial auctioneers are most likely to have the best bargains – and are less likely to be demanding a buyers' premium. But do plan ahead before turning up to a wine auction. Get a catalogue, which you may have to pay for, a couple of days in advance, and decide which lots you would like to bid for, and up to what price – beyond which you should resolve not to stray. The biggest savings are usually to be had on the biggest lots, so it can be sensible to form a syndicate of two or more cheap-wine buffs to bid for and subsequently divide up a large lot of several cases.

Check in the catalogue exactly what you will be letting yourself in for. Some lots will be subject to VAT and some will not – this should be stated in the catalogue. Not all the lots will be lurking in the auctioneer's back rooms, and there may therefore be a delivery charge to take into account.

Some auction houses will arrange preview tastings of the wines on offer. These are well worth attending, as you must otherwise buy the wine purely on the basis of the auctioneer's scanty description. And if the wine you buy turns out to be vile, the auctioneer will quote *caveat emptor* ('buyer beware'), which means, in effect, tough luck.

Duff Bottles

Buying wine from a merchant, whether it's the local supermarket or the most chic purveyor of noble clarets, entitles you to goods of merchantable quality. When it comes to wine, this term tends to be open to all sorts of interpretations because the cheapest bottles can certainly prove less than wonderful to drink, and yet may well have no fault in them that would oblige the seller to refund the customer's money.

But how do you tell the difference between a wine that is genuinely bad – or *un*merchantable – and a wine that is simply not to your taste?

Some of the symptoms of completely duff wine are, mercifully, unmistakable. One is cloudiness; all wine must be crystal clear to be drinkable (yes, ancient ports and the like will cloud up a bit if given a good shake, but no everyday table wine should). A second bad sign is a taste of corkiness – in which the dusty, mouldy-wood taint of cork is actually imparted into the flavour of the wine. This is becoming an increasingly common fault in wine, because the quality of corks is in decline. If you buy a case of any given wine and the first bottle tastes corky, it's quite likely the other eleven will be similarly revolting – as bad corks tend to come in batches.

Do not confuse the 'corky' defect with the commonly quoted fault of 'corked'. The term corked is used very generally for any wine that tastes a bit off, but most particularly for the bottle which has oxidized because air has got into it – via the cork. Such a wine will have a flat, musty smell and a flavour to match; it may well taste very akin to vinegar, and the bottle's inside may be coated with a substance rather like the tea stain in an unwashed cup.

A bottle of wine exhibiting any of these nasty

characteristics should go straight back to the shop, accompanied by the other bottles if you bought more than one of the same variety. Either demand your money back or ask for a replacement bottle. But don't ask for another bottle of the same wine, as the chances are all too good that it will be just as bad.

Decent retailers – or wine bar or restaurant managers – should not demur, as all they have to do is demand recompense from whoever sold them the duff wine in the first place.

What you cannot do, by rights, is to return a bottle that is in good condition but which you don't like. To this extent, discovering new wines can be a risky business – although some merchants, particularly the 'warehouse' ones, do now offer regular tastings of wines to potential customers.

The wine trade as a whole is not unaware of the hazards of choosing the right wine aided only by an indecipherable label. To help shoppers discriminate between different styles of wine, many merchants and supermarkets have adopted identification systems, usually based on simple symbols. In Sainsbury's and Tesco, Peter Dominic and Victoria Wine, for example, you will find all white wines are identified by a number from 1 to 9 to indicate dryness or sweetness. The sweeter the wine, the higher the number.

Red wines are a bit trickier. Nevertheless, the Wine Development Board – the trade association which does public relations for the British wine business as a whole – has come up with a basic guide to the different styles, and this has already been adopted by a good many merchants. Reds are identified by one of five letters from A to E. Each indicates a style approximately as follows:

A   Light, slurping wines. These may be dry, like Bardolino, or sweetish, like most Lambrusco. They should be cheap, and may be nasty!

B   Wines with a bit more body, but still on the light side. They will most likely be dry. Examples are Navarra (from Spain) and Côtes du Roussillon (from deepest south-west France). These can be cheap, and very good value, especially from supermarkets.

C   The popular wines of Bordeaux, the Côtes du Rhône and Rioja largely fall into this category. 'Medium-bodied' might be a fair description. But don't expect to find many decent bottles of this type under £3.

D   Alcoholic (12 degrees or more), meaty red wines with dark colour and lots of flavour. These include bargain wines such as Dão (from Portugal) and Bulgarian Cabernet Sauvignon.

E   Really soupy, heavy red wines such as Italy's famous – but never cheap – Barolo and the headache-prompting red plonks of Greece. Don't expect anything brilliant under £3 from this group.

Label Language

The labels on the bottle themselves offer helpful information to a varying degree. More and more wines are now sold with helpful back labels which do often give quite a detailed account of the contents. Tesco own-label Bairrada, a Portuguese red that is one of the very best buys of all, for example, carries on its main label merely the somewhat obvious information that its contents consist of 'Vinho Tinto – Red Wine' and the usual bottle size, vintage and alcoholic strength.

Turn to the back label, however, and you learn that

'The defined region of Bairrada lies to the south of the city of Oporto.' Yes, you can take or leave such information, but there's more: 'This full bodied, smooth wine has a pleasant character and is suitable for most meat dishes. Serve at room temperature.' It is a helpful, if incomplete, description of a wine with which most shoppers are no doubt unfamiliar.

So, always read the back label, if there is one. If there isn't, what can be gleaned from the front? Sadly, precious little – especially among cheaper wines. But there are some key words and phrases to look out for –

Abboccato   Italian for slightly sweet – commonly so slightly that the wine in question can appear quite dry, but with a mildly fruity overtone. The popular white wines of Orvieto are usually graded *abboccato* – avoid *secco* ('dry') Orvieto, which is generally nasty.

Amabile   Italian again, this implies some degree of sweetness in the wine, but not as much as *dolce*.

Appellation contrôlée   The proud boast on 'quality' French wine that the contents of the bottle are guaranteed to conform to the origin, vintage and so on as stated on the label. AC is a dependable reassurance of authenticity, but there is no guarantee that you will either like the wine or consider it good value.

Brut   Very dry, as in sparkling wines.

Clarete   Portuguese and Spanish term for the lighter red wines.

Classico   This describes wine from what are reputed to be the best growing areas of the various Italian wine regions. Accordingly, winemakers in the *Classico* district of Tuscany style their produce 'Chianti Classico'. Wines so designated may well be of good quality, but that does not exclude those labelled simply with the generic name – such as plain old 'Chianti' – from being good wines too.

Denominación de Origen   Spain's equivalent of *appellation contrôlée*.

Denominazione di Origine Controllata   Ditto for Italy.

Doce, Dolce, Doux, Dulce   Sweet – and probably sticky.

Grand Vin   Meaningless French hype if applied to any bottle costing under £3.

Grape varieties   More and more wines, particularly cheaper ones, are now labelled simply with the grape variety from which they are made. Under wine laws, the named variety must make up at least half the content of the bottle, so you can reasonably expect the wine to have some identifiable characteristics. The grapes most likely to make an appearance on labels are:

Cabernet Sauvignon – the classic red wine grape of Bordeaux, but also widely grown in less trendy climes – such as Bulgaria, Romania, Chile and the United States. To be drinkable, Cabernet Sauvignon needs a bit of age, then it becomes round, smooth and delicious. Best bargain example is the Bulgarian Cabernet now widely on sale from the 1981 vintage, and costing only about £2.

Chardonnay – the white grape that goes into the ridiculously overpriced white wines of Burgundy, this variety is also widely grown elsewhere. Bulgaria, Italy and Spain are making decent wines with it. Characteristics are an apple-scented dryness and, in the pricier wines, a 'buttery' smell and flavour. At the cheap level, you can expect a fresh, quite complex dry white wine – sometimes of real quality.

Gamay – this is the grape that goes into all those oceans of Beaujolais that pour in every November, getting progressively more expensive every year. But Gamay grapes are grown elsewhere, mainly in other regions of France, and these 'mock-Beaujolais' wines can represent better value than the real thing. Expect a light, freshly fruity red wine.

Merlot – extensively grown in Bordeaux, Merlot is the grape blended with Cabernet Sauvignon to 'soften' the overall mix. On its own, it makes a soft, juicy red wine that is ready for drinking at a young age. Look out for low-cost Italian Merlot.

Muscat – a white grape producing intensely sweet, table-grape-flavoured wines. But note an exception: Muscat wine from Alsace is dry.

Riesling – the grape that goes into the best German wines – and, in limited quantities, into some of the worst German wines as well – has an imitator whose name frequently appears on cheap Eastern bloc wines. This pseudo-Riesling is variously known as Welschriesling or Italian Riesling and, most famously, as Laski Riesling – the Yugoslav medium white wine that still tops the wine-sales charts in Britain. From non-German bottles labelled Riesling, expect a slightly bland, grapey medium-dry wine. An exception is the deliciously crisp, fruity and aromatic 'Rhine Riesling' from the Barossa Valley in South Australia. Regrettably, there is little of this nectar about at under £3. Final word on Riesling: it is pronounced *Reez*ling NOT *Rye*sling!

Sauvignon – probably the grape name that most commonly appears on labels. The wine is likely to be very dry and rather light, especially under £3. White wine only.

Syrah – this is the grape that makes the best red Rhône wines, but grown elsewhere it does very well. Syrah from the deep south of France can be excellent, and very cheap. The grape is known as Shiraz in Australia, where it produces hearty, even spicy red wines – particularly when blended with Cabernet Sauvignon. There are occasional Aussie bargains based on these grapes at under £3.

Kabinett   German term for a quality wine that has been made without the addition of sugar to bring it up to sufficient strength. A step up from *QbA*. Many excellent *Kabinett* wines are actually cheaper than the inferior, branded Liebfraumilch concoctions.

Mousseux   An indication, mainly on cheaper wines, that the contents of the bottle are fizzy.

Pétillant   An indication that the contents are very slightly fizzy.

QbA   Stands   for   *Qualitätswein   bestimmter Anbaugebiete*, this is broadly the German equivalent of *appellation contrôlée*.

QmP   Stands for *Qualitätswein mit Prädikat*, a class of German wines that are a cut above the bog-standard *QbA* types. There are five grades of *QmP* wines, the basic one being *Kabinett* and the next in line being *Spätlese*. The posher ranks are never seen at under £3.

Reserva, Riserva   Wine (usually from Italy, Portugal or Spain) that has been aged a while. The presence of the term does not necessarily indicate better quality – just that the wine is older.

Sec, Secco, Seco   Dry.

Spätlese   German for 'late-picked', it means the

grapes that went into the wine should have had a slightly more concentrated sweetness after being left for as long as possible on the vine. *Spätlese* wines can be found under £3, and are worth seeking out.

Superiore Italian term for a wine that qualifies to a rank above its neighbours because it has more age, or more alcohol – not necessarily because it tastes any better.

Sur lie A term appended to Muscadet, the bone-dry white wine of the Loire valley in France – which implies that it will have a slightly more aromatic and richer character because it was left in the barrel 'on the lees' (the yeasty detritus from fermentation) right up to the time it was bottled. Trouble is, *sur lie* Muscadets tend to be more expensive, and you need to be a veritable *aficionado* to spot the distinction between those with and those without.

Tafelwein German *vin ordinaire* – not often seen in Britain.

Tinto Term for the heftier red wines of Portugal and Spain.

Vin de pays French country wine – and a name worth watching for, as many of the best bargains are sold under this name, which implies wine of a quality a step up from basic plonk, but too humble for the accolade of *appellation contrôlée*.

Vin de table, Vino de tavola, Vino do mesa - Table wine – in other words, plonk.

Two

700 Wines Under £3

The principal purpose of this little guide is to direct shoppers to the many delicious wines that lurk at the less extravagant end of the price scale. The wines mentioned in the following pages are all cheap, but quality does vary. As well as the brief notes about the style of wine – dry or sweet, light or heady and so on – each one has a quality grading of one, two, three or four stars. These grades, which are awarded on a purely subjective basis by the author, can be interpreted as follows:

    ★   Basic plonk but good value at the price
  ★★   Good-quality wine at a fair price
★★★   Good-quality wine at a bargain price
★★★★   Only a very few wines receive this accolade – it signifies a wine of exceptional class that would probably be a bargain at twice the price

The wines that do appear in the listings are the *good* ones. I have tasted a vast number of sub-£3 bottles during the last two years in preparing this book, and many hundreds have turned out to be either poor value even at a low price – or simply downright vile. I have resisted the temptation to devote space to the worst offenders, largely because one tasting can prove insufficient grounds upon which to condemn a wine. It might have been an untypically bad bottle – or perhaps just a bad day for the taster!

It is a limitation of a guide such as this that it remains up to date for only a short time. Some of the wines mentioned in the listings will, inevitably, have been sold out by the time you, the reader, discover them in these pages. Prices change, too, so those given can only be regarded as a guide, not as definitive.

To minimize these hazards, all stockists mentioned for the wines were contacted shortly before the book went to press – at which time all the prices listed here were confirmed, as was the expected availability of the wines.

That's the disclaimers dealt with! Now to the listings. Within the various sections, the wines appear under the name most prominently stated on their labels. Irritatingly, many wines have ridiculously complicated and lengthy names. What's more, the longest names seem to be the least helpful in terms of describing the contents of the bottle.

Consequently, long-windedly named wines may appear under more than one heading in the listings, in case the true name is a little difficult to extract from all the other wording. Cross-references will direct you to the main entry.

The listings are based on a simple A to Z principle and

are not subdivided into countries of origin. This is simply because it is not, for the purposes of this guide, the source of the wine that counts, but the merits of the wine itself.

Details of all the stockists mentioned in the listings appear on page 155.

White Wines Under £3

These include dry, medium and sweet whites. Sparkling wines are covered in the section beginning on page 149.

Alcohol-free wine   *See* Eisberg and Masson.

Alsace   North-eastern French province producing mainly expensive fine wines with German-sounding names (from the German grape varieties used in them), but in the dry style of French wine rather than the grapey, 'soft' Teutonic manner. Cheap Alsace wines are scarce, but there are drinkable exceptions.
Sainsbury's Alsace Pinot Blanc★ £2.65, a French grape, dry and fresh.
Sainsbury's Sylvaner d'Alsace★★ £2.85, dry but quite grapey.
Tesco Alsace Pinot Blanc★ £2.69, clean-tasting, refreshing.
Vin d'Alsace Sylvaner 1985 Reserve St Hippolyte★★ £2.69, Majestic, also grapey-dry.

Anjou   Region encompassing several classy wine-growing districts just to the south of the river Loire in western France. The cheap white wines are simply called

Anjou Blanc, are generally medium-dry rather than bone-dry, and come from one grape, the Chenin Blanc. *Anjou Blanc Chéreau Carré*★ £2.80, Dolamore.

Alsace

This picturesque province of north-east France, lying between the Vosges mountains and the river Rhine, produces delicious white wines which combine the charms of French winemaking with the solid virtues of German grapes. Alsace wines are nearly all sold under the name of the grapes that go into them: **Gewürztraminer**, **Riesling** and **Sylvaner**, for example.

But while these wines come in tall, slim, green *flute* bottles – closely resembling Mosel – they are quite unlike the sweet, soft produce of Germany. Alsace wines are commonly very dry in character, but with exotic and exciting flavours and aromas.

Alsace wine has never been cheap, but there are a few good bottles to be found at under £3 – particularly in supermarkets (notably Sainsbury's). A new addition to the Alsace grape menu is the **Pinot Blanc** – not just reassuringly French in name but also capable of making very gulpable low-cost everyday wine. Perhaps the most interesting Alsace wine, however, is the spicy and exotic dry white from the Gewürztraminer grape.

Morgan Furze Anjou Blanc★ £1.99, Peter Dominic, slightly sweet.
Sainsbury's Blanc Anjou★ £1.85.
Tesco Anjou Blanc★ £1.99.

Aveleda   Brand-name for one of the more popular *vinho verde* wines from Portugal. *See* Vinho verde.

Austria

The non-freezing wines that made western Europe's least loved nation even more of a laughing stock were all of the sweeter, costlier – and therefore more worth doctoring – variety. Nevertheless, cheap Austrian wines have pretty well disappeared along with the dodgy expensive ones, leaving only a ramshackle selection for forgiving Austrophiles to choose from. (See **Schluck** and **Grüner Veltliner**.)

Australia

Aussie wines are very good indeed, but Aussie wines under £3 are, sadly, about as scarce as flying kangaroos. The excellent London merchant, Alex Findlater, who lists more than 200 different wines from the Antipodes, has a few around the magic mark. Oddbins shops make a speciality of Australia, too, and do have some sub-£3 rarities.

Bergerac Not only the Jersey detective hero who never touches the stuff, but also the wine from the Dordogne district of the same name just east of Bordeaux in south-west France. Bergerac makes some good sweet whites (*see* Monbazillac), as well as some very good cheap dry ones, characterized by a fresh smell and crisp flavour.

Asda Bergerac Blanc★ £1.95.
Blanc de Blanc AC Bergerac, Domaine des Templiers★★ £2.85, Willoughbys.
Sainsbury's Bergerac Blanc★ £2.15.
Tesco Bergerac Blanc★★ £2.19.

Bernkastel A well-known *Bereich* (wine-growing district) of the Mosel, to the south of Bonn in Germany. Just as with other famous *Bereichen*, such as Nierstein and Piesport, Bernkastel churns out vast quantities of ordinary (QbA) wine under its generic name – or variations of it. Quality is pretty consistent and the style of the wine is softly grapey and medium-dry. As with all Mosel, the wines come in green bottles.

Bereich Bernkastel Drathen 1986★ £1.95, Oddbins.
Bereich Bernkastel Riesling 1985 Langenbach★ £2.69, Thresher.
Bereich Bernkastel Riesling Schneider 1983/4★ £2.65, Willoughbys.
Lohengrin Bernkasteler Kurfürstlay★ £2.15, Co-op.
Sainsbury's Bernkasteler Kurfürstlay Qba★★ £2.25.
Tesco Bernkastel★★ £2.29.
Waitrose Bereich Bernkastel 1985★ £2.25.

Bianco di Custoza A really toothsome dry white wine in the style of the best Soave, from near Verona in northern Italy. Strongly recommended.

Tesco Bianco di Custoza★★★ £2.29.

Bianco di Custoza
DENOMINAZIONE DI ORIGINE CONTROLLATA
PRODUCE OF ITALY
70 cl ℮ SELECTED FOR TESCO 12% vol
SERVE CHILLED
BOTTLED BY LAGARIAVINI S.p.A.- VOLANO (TRENTO) ITALY

Blanc de blancs French wine producers seem to believe that this term has some particular drawing power when writ large on labels. It means white wine made from white (well, green) grapes, as opposed to black grapes. This has no bearing on the quality of the wine whatever and many of the greatest white wines are made at least partly from black grapes – champagne, for instance.

Many good wines bear the *blanc de blancs* description (*see* Bergerac and Bordeaux, for example), and all kinds of cheap plonks are sold under the label, too – many of them horrible, but some rather better.

Blanc de Blancs Vin de Pays de la Vallée de Paradis★★ £2.30 Adnams/£2.23 Lay & Wheeler, crispy-dry.

29

Blanc de Blancs Vin de Table Henri Lambert★ £1.95,
Majestic, dry and delicate.
Tesco Blanc de Blancs★★ £1.79, fresh, good value.

Bordeaux blanc France's most celebrated winemak-
ing region trades largely on its red wine, or 'claret' as we
often call it in Britain. But Bordeaux also produces fine
whites such as the honeyed and luscious 'pudding'
Sauternes and Barsacs. There are some interesting dry
whites as well, and it is really only among these that
cheap buys are to be found.
Asda Bordeaux Blanc★ £1.99.
Bordeaux Blanc★ £2.19, Waitrose.
Bordeaux Blanc Jules Lenaire★ £2.49, Roberts and
Cooper.
Bordeaux Blanc Sec Peter Sichel★★ £1.99, Majestic.
Bordeaux Sec 1985 Barton & Guestier★ £1.98, Oddbins.
La Tourelle Bordeaux Blanc★ £2.85, Peter Dominic.
Sainsbury's Bordeaux Blanc★ £2.09.
Tesco Bordeaux Blanc★ £2.19.

Bucelas Faintly oily but deliciously flavoured dry
white Portuguese wine – an acquired taste well worth
discovering; good with food.
Bucelas Velho 1983 Caves Velhas★★ £2.79, Oddbins.

Bulgaria At the last count there were nine different
white wines from Bulgaria on sale here, all of them
extraordinarily cheap. Most go under their 'varietal'
name (that of the grape variety from which they are
largely or entirely made), so *see* separate entries for Chardonnay, Riesling and Sauvignon. There are three wines
made from a blend of grapes as really cheap, basic whites.
These are marketed either under their own, Bulgarian
brand name of Mehana or behind retailers' own labels.

British Wine

There is an important distinction between 'English' wine and 'British' wine. The former is made from grapes grown in England and Wales – and much of it is very good indeed, though not generally cheap. So-called 'British' wine is quite different. It is made from grape concentrates imported from abroad (mainly from Italy) which are fermented into wine in factories here.

Well-known brands of British wine such as Wincarnis – celebrating its glorious centenary in 1987 – have long been sold as tonics, whereas newer varieties such as Concorde and Moussec trade on their low prices. But these wines are really only marginally less expensive than the cheapest plonks from perfectly respectable continental growers. For sheer value, supermarket Spanish or Eastern European wines at around £2.00 look a much better buy than British confections at just a few pence less.

Bulgarian White★★ £1.69 Asda/Majestic/£1.79 Waitrose, medium-dry.
Mehana Bulgarian Dry White Wine★★ £1.65, Oddbins, fresh and crisp.
Mehana Bulgarian Medium Dry White Wine★★ £1.89, Peter Dominic/Thresher.
Mehana Bulgarian Sweet White Wine★★ £1.65, Oddbins, rich but not sticky.

California   Top-quality American wines are fine, and expensive. The cheaper ones are rather less exciting. But a few exceptions still crop up (*see also* Masson).
California White★ £2.55, Majestic, medium-dry.
Californian White★ £2.55, Peter Dominic.
Sainsbury's Californian★ £2.35, medium-dry.

United States

Wine writers trumpet the brilliance of America's winemakers above all others. The catch is that, like most of the much-written-about wines, they ain't cheap. Drinkable American wine under £3 is in very short supply.

Cante-Cigale   Name under which a group of very handy winemakers of the Hérault district of southern France produce several fine red and white wines.
Cante-Cigale 1985/6 Vin de Pays de l'Hérault★★ £2.25, Waitrose, dry and freshly delicious.

Chardonnay   An upmarket grape variety that makes some of the very grandest white wines, including burgundies and champagnes. It flourishes in the New World, and American and Australian 'varietal' Chardonnays are highly prized. But Chardonnays don't come cheap, except from Eastern European vineyards.
These humble wines are great value: fresh, appley and zesty.
Chardonnay Khan Krum 1983★★★ £2.59 Majestic/ Oddbins.

Bulgarian Chardonnay★★★ £2.09 Gough Brothers/
Majestic/£2.05 Oddbins.
Safeway Hungarian Chardonnay★★ £1.85.

Charente This region of south-west France is best
known for Cognac, the world-famous brandy which
owes its origins to the fact that Charente wine was so
awful that someone decided to distil it – and *voilà*,
wonderful spirit by sheer chance. This tale is probably
rubbish, though, and there are even one or two good dry
white wines.
Sainsbury's Vin de Pays des Charentes★ £1.89.
Vin de Pays Charentais 1986 Gaston Sylvain★★ £2.25,
Waitrose.

Chenin blanc Grape variety widely grown in
France's Loire valley. It can make delicious wines but
also some rather dull, flat-tasting ones. The better dry
whites are good value.
Chenin Blanc 1984/5 KWV★ £2.49, Waitrose, South
African dry.
Chenin Blanc Touraine 1985★ £2.65, Waitrose,
medium-dry.
Chenin Blanc Vin Touchais 1985★ £1.99, Majestic, full,
lingering flavour.
Chenin 1986 Vin de Pays R. Pannier★ £1.95, Oddbins.
Tesco Vin de Pays Chenin Blanc★ £1.89.

Chiddingstone English wine from a quirky Kent
vineyard.
Chiddingstone★★ £2.99, Peter Dominic, fresh and
aromatic.

Colli Albani The name means Alban Hills in Italian.
The wine is the fragrant, crisp dry white from the said
hills, just south of Rome, where Frascati is made.

Tesco Colli Albani★★★ 1.5 litres £3.59. (Only sold in this jumbo-size; equivalent price for a 70cl bottle would be £1.68 – remarkable value.)

Colombard Light, dry, fresh white from southern France; the name is that of the grape that makes the wine.
Colombard Vin de Pays Côtes de Gascogne Plaimont★★ £2.65 Adnams/£2.49 Lay & Wheeler.

Cooks New Zealand winemaker producing several good wines including a couple of modestly priced ones.
Cooks Dry White★ £2.99, Thresher.

Corbières Region of the Aude in France's deep south, better-famed for gutsy red wines. But a few good, cheap dry whites are made too.
Asda Corbières Blanc★ £1.99.
Corbières AC 1986★ £2.15, Waitrose.

Corrida   Big-selling Spanish branded wine of no spe-
cial distinction, but cheap.
Corrida Dry White★ £1.99, Thresher.
Corrida Medium Dry White★ £1.99, Thresher.
Corrida Sweet White★ £1.99, Thresher.

Coteaux du Layon   The name means the hillsides of
Layon, a district of Anjou in France's Loire valley where
they make very good, sweetish white wines which are usually rather expensive. There is an honourable exception.
Coteaux du Layon AC★★ £2.25, Waitrose.

Côtes   Where a French wine begins its name with
Côtes du this-or-that, we are supposed to assume that
the stuff will be superior because the grapes were grown
in hillside vineyards; and as any wine bore will tell you,
slopes (*côtes*) reputedly make for better grapes than flat
areas. Much of the time, in fact, the *côtes* part of a wine's
name has no significance whatever. But there are plenty
of decent, cheap wines with this woolly prefix.

   First, some sweet wines, three from the impressive-
sounding Premières Côtes de Bordeaux which lie well
away from the trendy centre of the famous region, but
turn out a nice line in low-cost 'dessert' wines. Also one
from another Bordeaux outpost, Côtes de Bergerac (*see
also* Bergerac).
Asda Côtes de Bergerac★ £1.95.
Premières Côtes de Bordeaux★ £2.45, Waitrose.
Premières Côtes de Bordeaux 1984★ £2.19, Littlewoods.
Sainsbury's Premières Côtes de Bordeaux★★ £2.39.

   Second, drier whites from southern France's count-
less *côtes*.
Côtes de Gascogne Cépage Colombard Vin de Pays★
£2.49, Davisons.
Côtes de Gascogne 1985★ £1.99, Majestic.
Côtes du Rhône Marcel Baron★ £2.69, Peter Dominic.

Sainsbury's Côtes du Rhône Blanc★★★ £2.75.
Domaine Meste Duran 1985 Vin de Pays des Côtes de Gascogne★★ 1.5 litres £4.95, Sainsbury's. (Price is equivalent to £2.31 a 70cl bottle.)

Culemborg Brand-name for a straightforward dry South African white.
Culemborg Colombar 1985/6★ £2.15, Waitrose.

Cuvée d'Adrien Brand-name for a dry but fruity-flavoured *vin de table* from a grower called Adrien Bertaillan.
Cuvée d'Adrien★ £2.06, Lay & Wheeler.

Cuvée des Minimes Brand-name for a decent dry *vin de table* from the big Piat firm (better known for Beaujolais).
Cuvée des Minimes Blanc★ £2.49, Peter Dominic.

36

Dão In the sun-baked heartland of Portugal, this region of sandy hills and pine woods produces substantial, interesting dry white wines which go very well with food, but not so very well without it.

Dão Branco 1981 Caves Velhas★ £2.59, Peter Dominic.
Dão Dom Ferraz 1982★ £2.69, Thresher.
Dão Grao Vasco Branco 1984★★ £2.69, Majestic.

Deidesheimer Hofstück Deidesheim is a village in Germany's Rheinpfalz region where many of the best Rhine wines are made; Hofstück is the *Grosslage* (group of vineyards) from which the grapes come for making into wine at the village. German wines are usually expensive at this level, but this is an exception.

Deidesheimer Hofstück QbA★★★ £2.59, Tesco, a beautiful scent and fresh fruit flavour.

Demestica Best-known of all Greek dry whites, from the wine firm of Achaia-Clauss in the Peloponnese.

Demestica★ £2.49, Peter Dominic/other stockists.

Domaine d'Escoubes An exceptional, perfumed fresh dry wine from south-west France.
Domaine d'Escoubes Blanc★★★ £2.19, Tesco.

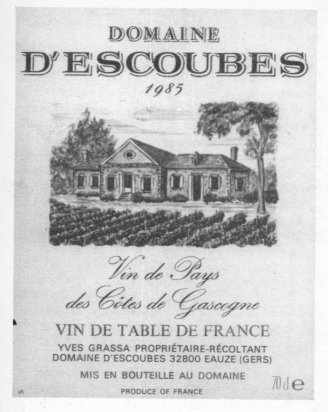

Dom Ferraz *See* Vinho verde.

Don Cortez A popular Spanish brand which comes in bottles of several sizes and a number of different flavours. The brand belongs to Grants of St James's and is therefore sold through Victoria Wine, which is also part of the Allied Lyons group. Unusually for a branded wine, it is not overpriced, and the quality is not too bad either.

Don Cortez Dry★★ £2.19, Victoria Wine, dry but with a hint of sweetness.

Don Cortez Medium Dry★ £2.19, Victoria Wine.

Don Cortez Sweet★ £2.19, Victoria Wine.

EEC Wine

The European wine lake is rising – and already lapping round the ankles of embarrassed Brussels bureaucrats. What to do with billions of litres of wine that nobody wants and yet which we have all as taxpayers paid for in subsidies?

Industrial alcohol is one answer. Another is EEC blended wine. So, off-licence shelves are now crowded with even more Gothic-scripted bottles of indeterminate wine at strangely low prices. Most EEC wine, be warned, is muck from Europe's leading overproducer, Italy, which has been tanked up with artificial preservatives and sweeteners and then bottled to look like German Hock (brown bottle) or Mosel (green bottle).

Look carefully at labels before buying what you think to be a German wine. If it doesn't say Produce of Germany it won't be German. It should confess to being a blend of wine from EEC countries if that is what it is – in which case avoid it!

Eisberg   What should be the cheapest of cheap wine, if only because it has no alcohol in it and therefore attracts no duty, turns out to be rather expensive. But this is one of the alcohol-free (well, almost, as it does have 0.05 per cent alcohol) wines that is just about palatable, tasting of slightly stale and watery German white, enlivened a little with a bit of carbonated fizz.
Eisberg Alcohol-Free Wine★ £1.65, Sainsbury's.

Entre-Deux-Mers   This extensive region east of Bordeaux in France is so named because it is bordered to the north by the river Dordogne and to the south by the river Garonne – hence 'between two seas'. Its reputation is for dry white wines, many of which are very good but by no means cheap. There are a few everyday, low-cost ones worth trying, but they should be as youthfully fresh as possible, so don't buy any vintage bottles pre-dating 1986.
Asda Entre-Deux-Mers★ £1.99.
Delpérier Entre-Deux-Mers★ £2.59, Peter Dominic.
Eschenauer Entre-Deux-Mers★ £2.89, Roberts and Cooper.
Tesco Entre-Deux-Mers★ £2.19.

España, Vino de   Few Spanish wines, even of the cheapest variety, dare describe themselves in such humble terms, but one excellent dry and cleanly fresh one does:
Sainsbury's Vino de España Blanco Seco★★★ £1.75.

Frascati   This is the everyday dry white wine of Rome's restaurants and cafes; it should be ripe-tasting and fresh, light and slurpable. Not much of the stuff we get in Britain could be thus described, but some of the wines have their charm.

France

For sheer quantities of wine, only Italy surpasses the productivity of the French *vignerons*; for quality, nobody does.

The basic French *vin ordinaire* or *vin de table* is not much in evidence here in Britain – it is not intended for export on any scale. The French wines that do appear here are graded in ascending order as *vin de pays* or, rather long-windedly, *vin délimité de qualité supérieure* (VDQS) or, top of the heap, *appellation contrôlée* (AC). The distinctions between these quality denotations are boring to a degree. Suffice it to say that any bottle bearing any of these designations has had to conform to at least minimum standards – which are applied both in the vineyard and in the winery.

French wines at the cheap end of the scale include many AC and VDQS bottles, while not all *vin de pays* is by any means either humble or inexpensive. As often as not, it is simple geography that denies first-class wines a more elevated official status; an estate owned by a genius of a winemaker in some vinous backwater without enough neighbouring vineyards to have attracted the authorities' attention will be *vin de pays* at best, however good its wine.

(For more detail about France's main wine-producing regions see the sections on Alsace, Bordeaux, Burgundy, Loire, Midi and Rhône.)

Carissa Frascati★★ £2.49, Co-op.
Frascati Cesari 1986★ £2.45, Majestic.
Frascati Rufinella 1985★★ £2.65, Waitrose.
Sainsbury's Frascati Secco Superiore★ £2.75.

French White   The notion that French wine must be
OK merely because it's French still has millions of
subscribers. Plenty of retailers consequently offer
ranges of wines simply labelled French White, Vin de
France Blanc and the like. These are the most basic of
wines, and very much a matter of personal taste;
perhaps what is most interesting about them compara-
tively is their prices. A few examples from respectable
stockists follow (note that figures in brackets are the
equivalent price for a 70cl bottle where only litres are on
sale).
Asda Vin de Table Dry White★ litre £2.25 (£1.57).
Sainsbury's Vin de France Dry★ litre £2.45 (£1.71).
St Michael French Dry White★ litre £3.25 (£2.27),
Marks & Spencer.
Tesco Vin Blanc★ litre carton £2.45 (£1.72).
Victoria Wine French Dry White★ £1.99.
Waitrose Vin Blanc★ litre £2.39 (£1.68).

Gambellara   Soave-style wine from near Verona in
northern Italy that outdoes the real thing for price and
comes very close for quality.
Tesco Gambellara Superiore★★ 1.5 litres £3.59 (£1.68
per 70cl).

Gatao   In spite of the nubile mermaid on the label, the
name of this very good vinho verde means 'cat'. *See*
Vinho verde.

Gewürztraminer   A name to be reckoned with. It is pronounced 'gehvoortstrahmeener' and is a variety of grape. Grown mainly in Alsace, Germany and Eastern Europe, this grape produces lovely scented, exotically flavoured dry white wine with a trace of spice. The wines are rarely cheap, but there is the odd welcome exception. *Safeway Yugoslav Gewürztraminer 1985*★★★ £2.15, good value.

Gros Plant   This French grape variety gives its name to a wine very much like Muscadet – bone dry, acidic but balanced up with fruitiness. The Gros Plant is the lighter style, and can be *too* acidic, but it is good with seafood, particularly *moules marinière*, and relatively cheap. *Gros Plant sur Lie Château de la Galissonière 1985*★★ £2.59, Peter Dominic.

Germany

Two-thirds of all the wine we drink in Britain is white, and of that about half is of the 'medium' – in other words slightly sweet – variety. Germany supplies more of this medium wine than any other source, most of it under what must be the best-known name in the business: **Liebfraumilch**.

German wine laws stipulate that Liebfraumilch must be made from certain types of grapes grown in specified regions of the Rhineland. This appears to provide scope for a full spectrum of quality from the undrinkable to the very drinkable – and all of it Liebfraumilch. The price of this wine seems to have little bearing on the quality either, so shopping for Liebfraumilch can be a chancy business – see the listings for some recommendations.

Happily, Germany produces other, better wine. Through the jumble of indecipherable Gothic script on the labels, look out for this phrase: *Qualitätswein mit Prädikat* or QmP (not to be confused with the even lengthier but much less reassuring designation *Qualitätswein bestimmter Anbaugebiete* or QbA). QmP signifies a German wine which has not been artificially sweetened, and indeed cheaper wines in this class are quite dry and usually ranked as *Kabinett* quality – many are quite delicious. Slightly sweeter *Spätlese* wines (late-picked, so the grapes have had a chance to ripen) are also available under £3 – that's cheaper than some big-name Liebfraumilch brands, and miles better value.

Grüner Veltliner   Reliable Austrian wine well worth trying as an alternative to German medium types.
Falkensteiner 1980 Grüner Veltliner Morandell★★ £2.70, Willoughbys.
Grants of St James's Grüner Veltliner★ £2.59, Victoria Wine.

Hérault   Highly productive – perhaps *over*productive – region of France's deep south to the west of the Rhône delta. Mostly rough reds but a few very cheap drinkable whites (*see also* Cante-Cigale).
Vin de Pays de l'Hérault Blanc★ £1.79, Majestic.

Hirondelle   One of the most famous, if not *the* most famous, branded wine ranges. But Hirondelle is not cheap. Best value is probably the 'pudding' wine.
Hirondelle Sweet White★ £2.59, Augustus Barnett.

Hock   Generic British name given to wine from the Rhine valley. Hock always comes in brown bottles, and allegedly gets its name from the Rhine town of Hochheim. Retailers' own-label Hocks have the general merit of being cheaper than Liebfraumilch, but not too much should be expected in the way of thrilling quality from such basic *Tafelwein*.

Bauer Deutscher Tafelwein Hock★ £1.79, Lay & Wheeler.
Sainsbury's Hock Deutscher Tafelwein★ £2.09.
St Michael Hock★ litre £2.99 (£2.10 per 70cl), Marks & Spencer.
Tesco Hock★ £1.69.

Hungary   Like Bulgaria – which has rather overtaken it as the leading Soviet-satellite wine producer – Hungary markets its wines under their varietal (grape) names. *See* Chardonnay and Olasz Riesling.

Jean d'Armes   It sounds like some daft French-policeman joke, but is in fact the name of a very cheap dry *vin de table*.
Jean d'Armes Blanc★ £1.69, Majestic.

Klüsserather St Michael   Good-quality Mosel wine from Germany, delicate with a lovely light grapey-sweet flavour, and amazing value.
Sainsbury's Klüsserather St Michael Spätlese 1983★★★ £2.79.

La Mancha   The vine-growing region of central Spain where our new EEC partner looks likeliest to launch its own wine lake. Certainly it is currently the source of Spain's cheapest plonk. The three listed are dry white.
Asda La Mancha★ £1.69.
Gran Verdad★ £1.99, Willoughbys.
Tesco La Mancha★ litre £2.19 (£1.53 per 70cl), *very* cheap wine.

Lambrusco   The white version of this frothy, sweet-ish wine from Italy's central Emilia-Romagna region is catching on almost as fast as its red partner. Wine bores sneer at the stuff, but this doesn't seem to interrupt its upwardly spiralling popularity. After all, it's cheap, it's fun, and if you like it, why not?

Carissa Lambrusco Bianco★ £1.89, Co-op.
Lambrusco Bianco Del Colle★ £2.39, Davisons.
Lambrusco White★ £2.16, Noble Grape.
Sainsbury's Lambrusco Bianco★ £1.98.
St Michael White Lambrusco★ £2.25, Marks & Spencer.
Tesco Lambrusco Bianco★ £1.79.

Laski Riesling The name of the grape which produces most of the white wine of Yugoslavia. It is quite different from the noble Riesling grown in Germany – and makes inferior wine, it must be said. The Laski has many synonyms, among them Welschriesling (nothing to do with Wales), Italico Riesling and Olasz Riesling.

Laski Riesling wine is, according to its importer, 'deservedly Britain's brand leading medium dry white wine'. The brand in question is Lutomer – named after

47

the district of Slovenia in Yugoslavia where the grapes are grown – but the Laski Riesling sold under retailers' own-labels is the same stuff. Shop around for best prices.

Lutomer Laski Riesling★ £2.25 Davisons/£2.19 Peter Dominic/£2.09 Sainsbury's/£2.19 Victoria Wine.

There are some good-value own-label bottles.

Sainsbury's Laski Riesling★ £1.85.

German Wine Labels – All you need to know

In Germany they like rules and they like numbers. These admirably upright instincts have applied themselves vigorously to the wine business – with the result that many a bottle label is nigh-on indecipherable.

How do you tell from the bottle and label what to expect from it if you cannot interpret all that Gothic wording and those cryptic numbers? Here are a few simple rules of thumb –

● A brown bottle means 'Hock' – wine from the Rhine valley – and a green one means a 'Mosel' – from, yes, the Mosel valley.
● The word *Tafelwein* means plonk; QbA means better plonk; QmP means posh wine.
● The more expensive a bottle is, the sweeter it is likely to be. (Though all wines under £3 are likely to be a 'medium', namely not-too-dry-not-too-sweet.)

● In the label's main wording, the first item will be the *bereich*, the main, defined wine-growing region whence the contents come. There may be a second name, that of the *grosslage* or village (or group of villages) within the *bereich* in question. Thus, a label may bear the simple name *Nierstein* or *Niersteiner Gütes Domthal* – the latter part of the name meaning the areas within the region, and not that the wine necessarily tastes *gut*!

● All the best German wines are made from Riesling grapes. If the word Riesling appears on the label, this is therefore a *gut* sign.

● 'Liebfraumilch' just means bland, medium Rhine wine.

● When you're paying under £3 a bottle, you can afford to ignore the jumble of numbers completely.

Tesco Laski Riesling ★ £1.79.
Thresher Laski Riesling ★ £1.99.
Victoria Wine Laski Riesling ★ £1.99.
Waitrose Laski Riesling ★ litre £2.49 (£1.74 per 70cl).

Liebfraumilch   In the seventeenth century, so we are told, an ecclesiastical vineyard at Liebfrauenstift near Worms in Germany's Rhineland was producing wine so divine that it was christened Liebfraumilch – 'the milk of Our Lady'.

The name caught on. Today, any wine of reasonable – but never high – standard made from a prescribed range of grape varieties from any one of four major vine-growing regions can call itself Liebfraumilch. About half the German wines sold in Britain carry the name; that's about 100 million bottles of Liebfraumilch a year.

Some of it is cheap. Cheaper, in fact, than it was five years ago. But some seems very expensive for what it is. Big-name brands such as Black Tower, Blue Nun and Goldener Oktober, for example, are rarely if ever offered under £3 a bottle and are quite commonly sold at over £4.

Liebfraumilch lovers need not despair, though, for price seems to have little bearing on quality. Own-label, low-cost Liebfraumilch is plentiful, particularly in the better supermarkets. The prices listed below speak for themselves.

Asda Liebfraumilch★ £1.75.

Drathen Liebfraumilch★ £1.85, Oddbins.

Littlewoods Liebfraumilch, Scholl & Hillebrand★★ £1.99.

Safeway Liebfraumilch★★ £1.99.
Sainsbury's Liebfraumilch★ £1.75.
St Dominic Liebfraumilch★ £2.19, Peter Dominic.
St Michael Liebfraumilch★ £2.35, Marks & Spencer.
Schloss Königin Liebfraumilch★ £1.69, Gateway.
Tesco Liebfraumilch★★ £1.69.
Victoria Wine Liebfraumilch★ £2.29.
Waitrose Liebfraumilch 1986★ £1.95.

Lutomer   Yugoslav brand-name. *See* Laski and Tiger Milk.

Masson   Paul Masson is the best-known of all the Californian wine producers and, remarkably, continues to sell wine here at reasonable prices.
Paul Masson California Carafe Dry White★ £2.89, Peter Dominic, reasonably fresh and fruity.
Paul Masson California Carafe★ £2.89 Peter Dominic/ £2.59 Oddbins, medium-dry.
Masson Light★ £1.89 Oddbins/£1.75 Sainsbury's, 'de-alcoholized' wine – this is probably the best of the non-alcoholic wines on the market, though not the cheapest; off-dry and some fruit flavour.

Mehana   Bulgarian brand-name. *See* Bulgaria.

Minervois   Superior district of the Midi in southern France famed mainly for red wines. A very few decent whites are made.
Domaine Maris Minervois 1985★★ £2.59, Majestic, dry and flavoursome.

Monbazillac   Sweet white wine of the Bergerac region next to Bordeaux. Good sweet wines are never cheap, but some Monbazillacs represent very good value.

Sainsbury's Monbazillac★★ £2.75, sweet but light, and a lovely colour.
Tesco Monbazillac★★ £2.75, a match for the Sainsbury one.

Sainsbury's
Monbazillac
Appellation Monbazillac Contrôlée
Sweet

Bottled in France for J Sainsbury plc Stamford Street
London SE1 9LL

by Union des Cooperatives Vinicoles de la Dordogne
(24) Saint-Laurent-des-Vignes (Dordogne) France

Alcohol 12% by volume 70 cl ℮

Produce of France

Mosel German wine region taking its name from the tributary of the Rhine in whose great valley the vineyards lie. The Mosel itself has two tributaries, the Saar and Ruwer, and the whole region is referred to as

Mosel–Saar–Ruwer on bottle labels. The bottles are green – distinguishing them from those of the Rhine, which are brown – and Mosel wines are said to be a little crisper and 'more elegant' than their brown-bottled counterparts. They are, nevertheless, medium-dry rather than bone-dry wines, and while more fun than Liebfraumilch, not really very different from the Hock of the Rhine – at the cheap end of the price scale, anyway. For wines from individual Mosel districts *see* Bernkastel, Klüsserather, Piesporter, Wiltinger and Zeller Schwartzer Katz.

Moselle Huesgen★ £2.39, Davisons.
Sainsbury's Landwein der Mosel★ litre carton £2.48 (£1.74 per 70cl).
Sainsbury's Moselle★ £2.09.
Tesco Moselle★ £1.79.

Tesco Moselle Saar Ruwer Riesling★★ £2.49, fine, fresh and clean-tasting.
Thresher Mosel★ £2.29.
Waitrose Mosel 1986★ £2.15.

Muscadet   The bone-dry and often rather acid white wine of the western reaches of the Loire river in France. The wine takes its name from the Muscadet grape, the vineyards for which extend almost to the Atlantic coast. The best vineyards are said to be those in the Sèvre et Maine region.

Youth is an important factor in Muscadet. Crisp and fresh in the first year after the vintage, the wine goes

Loire

From the port of Nantes on the west coast, the mighty Loire river extends some 200 miles east into the heartland of France. Along the way, in the great green valley cut by the river, thousands of vineyards produce a delicious diversity of wines.

Common to these wines is a lightness of style – in the reds and rosés as well as the whites – and those in the trade often refer to the generic 'charm' of them. Many Loire wines, happily, have the additional appeal of being reasonably priced. Decent **Muscadet** can be found under £3 and **Anjou** wines, particularly the rosés, can be good value. Look out, too, for both red and white **Touraine** wines.

A few Loire wines have lately come into fashion to the extent that their prices have become exorbitant. Sancerre and Pouilly-Fumé are the worst examples, both of them respectable enough wines, but at the £5-plus prices now demanded for them, far too expensive.

into pretty rapid decline after its second Christmas. So buy the 1986 vintage in preference to any 1985 that might be left over. Some wines that have been a success in recent vintages are listed.

Asda Muscadet de Sèvre et Maine★ £2.09.

Grants of St James's Muscadet de Sèvre et Maine★ £2.89, Victoria Wine.

Muscadet Bouscades 1986★★ £2.15, Majestic.

Muscadet de Sèvre et Maine 1986, Cellier de la Roche★★ £2.74, Lay & Wheeler.

Muscadet de Sèvre et Maine Lacombe★ £2.59, Peter Dominic.

Muscadet La Noelle★ £2.49 Gough Brothers/£2.39 Oddbins.

Sainsbury's Muscadet de Sèvre et Maine★ £2.25.

Tesco Muscadet★ £2.29.

Muscat A grape variety grown just about everywhere in the world for its extra-sweet – and often distinctly sickly – wine. Good Muscat wines under £3 are rare indeed.

Muscat de Frontignan Cuvée José Sala★★ £2.69, Majestic.

Sainsbury's Moscatel de Valencia★ £2.45.

Navarra Neighbour to Rioja in the north of Spain, the Navarra region is fast gaining a reputation for its wines, and they are relatively cheap.

Bardon Larums Viura★★ £2.75, Sherston Wine Co., crispy dry.

Safeway Gran Feudo Navarra★ £2.15, crisp, light-weight.

Sainsbury's Navarra Seco 1984★ £2.19.

Senorio de Sarria Semi-Seco★★ £2.49, Arriba Kettle, enjoyably sweet and light.

Hungary

Land-locked and mysterious, Hungary is rightly renowned for all sorts of spicy and exotic food and drink. Private enterprise is gradually coming back to life in the general Soviet thaw and many small wine estates are making their own delicious wines.

Sadly these fine wines are not found here at the low prices that once would have prevailed – if they can be found here at all. Most Hungarian wine shipped to Britain is of modest quality, such as the **Olasz Riesling** that seems to be much favoured by the wine-box business. In box or bottle, it makes a pleasant medium white wine – but nothing exciting.

Hungary's best-known red wine is the so-called **Bull's Blood**, by reputation a hearty and slightly peppery-tasting number from the fortress town of Eger. Ripping yarns about ferocious Magyars quaffing the stuff as they slew medieval Turkish invaders have been artfully employed to enhance the wine's butch reputation – but you might have your doubts if you try the current vintage, which is disappointingly bland.

Nierstein A *Bereich* (wine-growing region) of the Rheinhessen in Germany, producing great quantities of everyday (QbA) wine either simply under its own name or under that of one of its *Grosslagen* (wine-making villages or group of villages), the best-known of which is Gütes Domthal. The wines are medium-dry and, at their best, grapey and freshly aromatic. They are really too delicate to appreciate with food (as are most German wines), but make a good aperitif.

Bereich Nierstein 1986 Drathen★ £2.19, Oddbins.

Bereich Nierstein Max B. W. Schmidt 1985★ £2.59, Davisons.

Bereich Nierstein St Charles★ £2.52, Dolamore.

Niersteiner Gütes Domthal★ £2.00, Noble Grape.

Niersteiner Gütes Domthal 1985★ £2.35, Majestic.

Sainsbury's Niersteiner Gütes Domthal★ £2.35.

St Michael Bereich Nierstein★ £2.65, Marks & Spencer.

Tesco Niersteiner Gütes Domthal★ £1.99.

Waitrose Bereich Nierstein 1986★ £2.29.

Olasz Riesling   Not Riesling as in the grape grown in Germany, but the Hungarian version of Laski Riesling (as grown in Yugoslavia). *See* Wine in Boxes on page 147.

Oppenheimer Krotenbrünnen   Typically long-winded German name for what can be a good Rhine wine. Oppenheim is an important town near Nierstein and Krotenbrünnen the great area of vineyards which supply the raw materials. The basic (QbA) wines are more interesting than Liebfraumilch, if less pronounce-able.

Oppenheimer Krotenbrünnen 1984★ £2.19, Peter Dominic.

Oppenheimer Krotenbrünnen Schneider 1984★ £2.57, Willoughbys.

Sainsbury's Oppenheimer Krotenbrünnen QmP Kabinett 1985★★ £2.75, grapey, superior flavour.

Tesco Oppenheimer Krotenbrünnen★ £2.09.

PRODUCE OF GERMANY

OPPENHEIMER KROTENBRUNNEN

Rheinhessen

QUALITÄTSWEIN b.A.

A. P. Nr. 4 906 022 078 85
SERVE CHILLED
SELECTED FOR TESCO
PRODUCED AND BOTTLED BY RÜDESHEIMER WEINKELLEREI GMBH,
RÜDESHEIM / RHEIN

70 cl e   9.5% vol

Orvieto Flavoursome and aromatic wine from Umbria in central Italy made in two styles, *abboccato* (slightly sweet) and *secco* (dry). All the best wines are *abboccato* – and rather expensive, but a couple of cheap ones are worth trying.
Safeway Orvieto Abboccato Cecchi★★ £2.79, 'herby' flavour, quite dry.
Tesco Orvieto Abboccato★ £2.49, quite dry.

Piesporter Michelsberg Piesport is a picturesque riverside village in Germany's Mosel valley. Michelsberg is the name given to the large expanse of neighbouring vineyard from which the local cheap-wine businesses get their grapes. The wines are standard lightweight Mosels, perhaps a little more delicate and less sugary in flavour than ordinary Liebfraumilch. Mysteriously, Piesporter Michelsberg tends to be more expensive than other Rhine and Mosel wines of no less elevated pedigree.

58

Piesporter Michelsberg 1986 Drathen★ £2.49, Oddbins.
Piesporter Michelsberg Zentralkellerei★ £2.59, Peter Dominic.
Sainsbury's Piesporter Michelsberg★ £2.49.
St Michael Piesporter Michelsberg★ £2.99, Marks & Spencer.
Tesco Piesporter Michelsberg★ £2.09.
Waitrose Piesporter Michelsberg★ £2.49.

Pinot Bianco   Grown with what must be positively Presbyterian economy in the Veneto region of northern

Italy, this is a grape variety which produces a very cheap, dry wine tending to the acidic, but drinkable all the same.

Sainsbury's Pinot Bianco del Veneto★ litre carton £2.25 (£1.57 per 70cl).

Pinot Blanc   Grape variety widely used in cheap Alsace wine. *See* Alsace.

Pinot Chardonnay   Exactly the same grape variety as Chardonnay. The name is used for some Hungarian Chardonnay wines.

Retsina   Greece's resinated dry white wine is quite a discovery on that first, cautious outing to the island taverna where the oiliness of the Aegean cuisine positively cries out for a grease-cutting glassful or five. Back home, it might be another story, especially as some Retsina seems rather more redolent of lavatory cleaner than it does of exotic Mediterranean resorts. It must be the pine they put in it.

For all that, Retsina is good wine in its own right, and for Graecophiles offers very good value. The wine is dry, with a curious combination of flavours, including lemon as well as pine. Best with taramasalata and other such fishy treats.

Corinth Retsina★ £2.15, Waitrose.
Metaxas Retsina★ £2.59, Davisons.
Retsina Achaia Clauss★ £2.39 Peter Dominic/£2.69 Willoughbys.
Retsina Kourtaki★★ £1.98 Sainsbury's/£2.30 Tanners.

Riesling   In this case, the 'Welsch' Riesling (*see also* Laski and Olasz Rieslings) as grown outside Germany. In Bulgaria it produces a pleasant, just off-dry wine with a good grapey flavour. It is marketed under various own-labels, but it's all the same thing.

Bulgarian Riesling★★ £2.05 Davisons/£2.17 Dolamore/ £1.85 Gough Brothers/£1.89 Majestic/£1.85 Oddbins/ £1.99 Peter Dominic/£2.09 Thresher.

Tesco Bulgarian Welsch Riesling★★ £1.89.

Victoria Wine Bulgarian Welsch Riesling★★ £2.15.

In Italy, the Riesling Italico (merely the local name for the Welsch) makes a medium-dry, cheapo wine with less charm than its Balkan counterpart.

Sainsbury's Riesling Italico★ 1.5 litres £3.85 (£1.80 per 70cl).

Tesco Riesling Italico★ 1.5 litres £3.79 (£1.77 per 70cl).

In Australia, they make a different wine altogether with the Riesling – in this case the same strain as the German or 'Rhine' variety. Australian Rieslings are crisply dry and fresh, and bonzer value.

Asda Australian Rhine Riesling★★ £2.35.

Barossa Valley Estate Rhine Riesling★★★ £2.49, Oddbins.

Murray River Riesling★★ £2.59, Peter Dominic.

Rioja Rightly famed for its 'oaky' red wines, this northern region of Spain produces some pretty fair whites, too. Some are made as fresh, light wines for drinking young; others are aged for a while in oak like their red counterparts. These latter wines are not to everyone's taste, as they can be rather hefty and oaky in flavour.

Banda Dorada Paternina Rioja★★ £2.99, Victoria Wine, oaky and dry.

Marqués de Cáceres Rioja★★ £2.89, Willoughbys, delicious, fresh, dry.

Olarra Rioja Anares 1985★ £2.49, Waitrose, oaky and dry.

Puerta Vieja Blanco 1984★ £2.69, Majestic, fresh but a bit acidic.
Tesco Rioja Vina Lanco★★★ £2.49, crisp and fresh, very good value.

Rock's   English 'country wine' can be loosely deemed to be potions fermented from the fruits of the hedge-rows. Of the very few made on a commercial basis, there is at least one worth a try.
Rock's Elderflower Wine 1984★ £2.49, Majestic, deli-cate dry white made with – of all things – gooseberries, and flavoured with elderflowers.

St Edmund   The name on what appears to be the only English wine – that is, wine made in England from

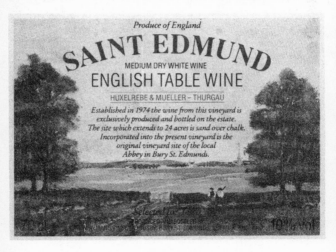

grapes grown in England – on sale at more than a couple of pence under £3.
St Edmund English Table Wine★ £2.49, Tesco.

England

English wine – made in England from grapes grown in England (and Wales) – is getting better and better. It is virtually all white and most of it is dry or medium-dry. The best is fresh, clean-tasting and scrumptiously fruity. But it is rarely cheap – winemakers here are obliged to pay duty just the same as their foreign rivals and, as most of the vineyards are very small, overheads are high.

The good news is that more and more vineyards are being planted; twenty years ago there were about ten acres altogether and now there are 1,200 acres. And the vines are beginning to get old enough to start producing decent grapes. So quality is on the up as well as quantity.

Maybe, just maybe, English wine will take off. So, fly the flag, buy a bottle of English – and help this marvellous and budding business on its way!

Saumur   Loire district making crispy dry whites.
Saumur Cuvée des Plantagenets Blanc★★ £2.79, Peter Dominic.

Sauvignon   White grape variety grown mainly in the Loire and Bordeaux regions of France, but also in Australia and more lately in Bulgaria. It makes fresh, dry wine which can be quite acidic, especially among the cheaper bottles. Best with fish dishes.

Bulgarian Sauvignon Blanc★★ £2.43 Dolamore/£1.99 Peter Dominic.

Sauvignon Blanc Cru des Vignerons★ £2.65, Peter Dominic.

Sauvignon Bordeaux Sec★ £2.29, Majestic.

Sauvignon de Touraine Guenauet 1984/5★ £2.70, Willoughbys.

Sauvignon de Touraine, Val de Loire★★ £2.35, Majestic.

Touraine Sauvignon Bougrier★ £2.34, Oddbins.

Schluck Good, fruity medium Austrian wine commonly sold at over £3.

Schluck★ £2.89, Victoria Wine.

Soave One of the really big Italian white wine names. At the cheap end of the scale, it is pretty ordinary dry wine for sloshing down with the *antipasti*. But some Soaves are better than others: look for the word 'Classico' on the label and go for the newest vintage.

Carissa Soave★★ £1.99, Co-op.

Littlewoods Soave★★ £2.09.

Soave Classico Lamberti★ £2.65, Peter Dominic.

Soave Classico Masi★★★ £2.83 Bibendum/£2.99 Oddbins.

Tesco Soave Classico★★★ £2.59.

   There are cheaper ordinary Soaves.

Sainsbury's Soave★ £2.09.

St Michael Soave★★ litre £3.25 (£2.28 per 70cl), Marks
& Spencer.

Soave Orsini★ £2.08, Noble Grape.

Soave Tadiello★ £1.89, Tanners.

Soave Gianni & Domenico★ £2.69 Davisons/£2.29
Roberts and Cooper.

Waitrose Soave 1986★ £1.95.

Tiger Milk   A mildly sweet curiosity from Yugoslavia that makes an enjoyably fruity aperitif wine.
Lutomer Ranina Tiger Milk★ £2.36, Willoughbys.

Tocai   White-grape variety that flourishes best in northern Italy to produce light, aromatic dry wines. There are various different strains of the grape – *see also* next entry.
Tesco Tocai del Piave★★ £1.89.
Tocai Cesari 1985★ £1.99, Majestic.

Sainsbury's
Tocai
Friulano Aquileia

Denominazione di Origine Controllata
Dry

Bottled in Italy for J Sainsbury plc Stamford Street London SE1 9LL
by Tenuta Ca' Bolani Acta Spa; 33052 Cervignano del Friuli, Italia

Produce
of Italy   Alcohol 11.5% by volume   70 cl ℮

Tocai Friulano   One of the variations of the Tocai grape, which has the distinction of producing an outstanding wine.

Sainsbury's Tocai Friulano Aquileia 1985★★★★ £2.69, classic, super-fine dry white with beautiful scents and aromas – adjective-defying! It is from the coastal Aquileia zone of Friuli–Venezia–Giulia in Italy's northeast.

Tonino   Branded wine from Sicily, medium-dry and decent value – but not always offered at a bargain price.
Tonino Vino Siciliano★ £1.99 Oddbins/£2.09 Thresher/ £2.54 Willoughbys.

Touraine   Winemaking region of France's Loire Valley. *See* Chenin Blanc and Sauvignon.

Trebbiano   The grape that goes, along with the Gambellara variety, into Italy's Soave (*see also* Gambellara). At Bologna, it makes a good, dry everyday plonk.
Sainsbury's Trebbiano di Romagna★ 1.5 litres £3.75 (£1.75 per 70cl).

Valdadige   The *vino da tavola* of Italy's northern-most wine-growing region's Adige river valley. Dry but quite fruity.
Tesco Valdadige Bianco★ £2.29.

Vaucluse   A *vin de pays* district of the Rhône delta in Mediterranean France. Produces a few decent dry whites.
Asda Vin de Pays de Vaucluse★ £1.85.
Safeway Vin de Vaucluse Blanc★ £1.99.
Vin de Pays de Vaucluse Blanc la Demoiselle★ litre £2.99 (£2.09 per 70cl), Peter Dominic.
Vin de Pays Vaucluse Blanc, Celliers de Marrenon★ £2.25, Davisons.

Verdicchio   The name of a pale-green grape variety which grows only in the Marches, a central province on Italy's Adriatic side. It makes very pale dry white wine with a delicate and unique flavour. The Verdicchio we get in Britain is mostly from the Castelli di Jesi area – a beautiful hilly landscape which takes its name from the town of Jesi and the old hill fortresses (*castelli*) around it. The wine is well known for its rather eccentric green amphora-shaped bottles.
Sainsbury's Verdicchio dei Castelli di Jesi Classico★★ £2.45.
Tesco Verdicchio Classico★ £2.49.
Verdicchio dei Castelli di Jesi Classico Garofoli★★ £2.91, Willoughbys.

Verdicchio dei Castelli di Jesi Lamberti★ £2.69, Peter Dominic.
Verdicchio dei Castelli di Jesi 1985★ £2.75, Waitrose.
Verdicchio dei Castello★ £2.75, Noble Grape.

Verduzzo del Piave Verduzzo is the grape variety, Piave the river valley just above Venice in northern Italy where the vineyards are. The wine is at its crisp, refreshing best when young, so look for the latest vintage.
Sainsbury's Verduzzo del Piave★★★ £1.99.
Tesco Verduzzo del Piave★★ £1.99.

Vin de pays 'Country wine' of France. Some 130 French districts make wine which is entitled to call itself *vin de pays* – a step up from plain old *vin de table* and sometimes as good as *appellation contrôlée* wines. *See* Charente, Côtes, Hérault, Vaucluse.

Vinho verde Portugal's vastly popular 'green wine' has a lightness and liveliness all its own. Most of these wines are sweetened for the British market, but some are more authentically dry, as they are in Portugal. Prices are erratic but, happily, some of the best wines are among the cheapest.

Portugal

From lightest **vinho verde** to the most soupy and headache-guaranteeing port, our oldest ally and new recruit to the EEC produces a remarkably diverse collection of good wines. Many of them represent remarkable value, too.

The regions of **Bairrada** and **Dão** are responsible for the best low-cost red table wines. These are generally sold when they have had a couple or more years of ageing, and are known as *vinho maduro* (mature wine). Smooth and 'round' in flavour, they can be delicious, though sometimes a little unexciting. The best ones are very often sold under supermarket own-labels at bargain prices. Tesco's own Bairrada, for example, is outstandingly good.

Vinho verde means 'green wine' literally, but in Portugal merely describes any wine that is too young to class as *maduro*. The slightly fizzy and fairly dry white wine that has carved such a name for itself here is made specially for the British market in a sweetened version of the bone-dry white the Portuguese themselves drink. In fact, most *vinho verde* is red, but it is not exported. Holidaymakers who try it *in situ* should beware: the red stuff is harsh and raw, and something of an acquired taste – though it is a very good antidote to oily Portuguese food, as well as being extremely cheap.

Asda Vinho Verde★ £1.85.

Aveleda Vinho Verde★ £2.93, Willoughbys.

Dom Ferraz Vinho Verde★★ £2.95 Dolamore/£2.49 Roberts and Cooper/£2.15 Thresher/Waitrose, dry style.

Gatao Vinho Verde★★ £2.59, Victoria Wine.

Sainsbury's Vinho Verde★ £1.98.

St Michael Vinho Verde★ £2.50, Marks & Spencer.

Tesco Vinho Verde★ £2.15.

Verdegar Vinho Verde★ £2.05, Oddbins, dry style.

Verde Mar Vinho Verde★ £2.19, Majestic.

Vino da mesa It means simply 'table wine' in Spanish.

Safeway Vino da Mesa★★ £1.75, good, clean dry white, good value.

Yugoslavia

The biggest-selling brand of wine available in Britain hails from Yugoslavia: Lutomer **Laski Riesling**. It appears in all sorts of livery as supermarket and off-licence own-labels as well as under the labels of importers Teltscher Brothers, but it's all the same not-too-dry, not-too-sweet white wine. Prices vary dramatically, so shop around.

There are a few other Yugoslav wines, some rather more interesting and almost as cheap. See **Gewürztraminer** and **Merlot** among others.

Vouvray   Upmarket white from France's Loire valley. Rarely seen at under £3.
Vouvray 1985 Val de Loire ★★ £2.95, Majestic, almost rich in flavour but quite dry.

Wiltinger   The name on most of the good wine from Germany's Saar valley in the Mosel region. The wines are exceptionally clean-tasting and well balanced between freshness and grapeyness. Worth seeking out.
Sainsbury's Wiltinger Scharzberg QmP Kabinett★★★ £2.75.
Tesco Wiltinger Scharzberg QmP Kabinett 1983★★★ £2.59.

Zeller Schwartze Katz   Zell is a vast *bereich* of the Mosel, and Schwartze Katz (which means 'black cat') the name given to many of its wines – good basic Mosels.
Zeller Schwartze Katz Riesling JF Brems 1985 ★★ litre £2.99 (£2.10 per 70cl), Majestic.

Rosé Wines Under £3

Rosés are made by a number of different methods, but in essence the wine is made from black grapes, the skins of which are allowed to remain in contact with the juice for just long enough to impart the desired amount of colour into the finished product.

Pink wines are not currently enjoying the trendiness of twenty years or so ago, and prices are pretty low. Quality, however, is not generally all that high either. The principal charm of rosé is surely its colour – combined with the notion that it can be drunk with just about any kind of food.

Anjou The district of the Loire Valley in France whence comes more rosé than anywhere else in the world. The best of the wine is made from the Cabernet grape, so look for its name on Anjou labels.

Anjou Rosé Caves des Vignerons★ £1.99, Peter Dominic, slightly sweet.

Anjou Rosé Chéreau-Carré★ £2.73, Dolamore, medium.

Anjou Rosé Grants of St James's★ £2.59, Victoria Wine, medium-dry.

Anjou Rosé Supérieur Roger Gouin★ £2.29, Davisons, medium.

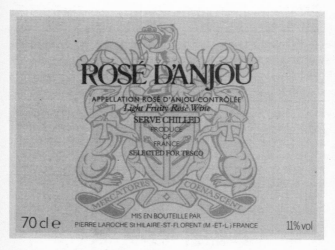

Asda Rosé d'Anjou★ £1.85, medium.

Rosé Cabernet d'Anjou Noel★★ £2.34, Willoughbys, medium-dry.

Rosé d'Anjou Maîtres Goustiers 1980★ £1.99, Majestic, medium-dry.

Rosé d'Anjou Gautier★ £2.49, Thresher, medium.

Rosé d'Anjou Marshall Taplow★ £2.49, Augustus Barnett, medium.
Rosé d'Anjou Les Celliers de la Loire★ £1.99, Tanners, medium.
Rosé d'Anjou Pierre Chaumont★ £2.09, Co-op, medium-sweet.
Safeway Cabernet d'Anjou Rosé★ £2.15.
Sainsbury's Rosé d'Anjou★ £1.99, medium.
St Michael Rosé d'Anjou★ litre £3.25 (£2.28 per 70cl), Marks & Spencer, medium.
Tesco Rosé d'Anjou★ £1.95, medium.

Bardolino This is one of Italy's best-known red wines – from near Verona in the northern Veneto region – and

there is one rosé variation of it, a lightweight, quite dry and likeable confection.
Tesco Chiaretto di Bardolino★★ £2.19.

Corrida Big brand-name from Spain.
Corrida Rosé★ £1.99, Thresher, quite sweet.

Dom Dias From Portugal, rather sweet.
Dom Dias Rosé Imperio★ £2.49 Davisons/£2.09 Peter Dominic.

Don Cortez Spanish brand, medium-dry.
Don Cortez Rosé★ £2.19, Victoria Wine.

French vin de table The cheapest pink plonks from indeterminate origins in France, but probably Anjou. Not for wine snobs. All medium.
Asda Vin de Table Rosé★ litre £2.29 (£1.60 per 70cl).
Choix du Roy Rosé Vin de Table★ litre £2.39 (£1.67 per 70cl), Tanners.
Sainsbury's Vin Rosé de France★ litre £2.45 (£1.72 per 70cl).
Tesco French Rosé★ litre £2.49 (£1.74 per 70cl).

Haut Poitou A trendy wine-growing district just outside the Anjou region that produces exceptional wines – though not cheaply. This one is dry, crisp and thoroughly delicious.
Cabernet Rosé du Haut Poitou 1985★★★ £2.89, Majestic.

Hérault Region of France's deep south better known for its reds, but the dry pink is just drinkable, especially at the price.
Vin de Pays de l'Hérault Rosé SOPR★ £1.79, Majestic.

LAMBRUSCO ROSÉ

VINO FRIZZANTE
A Semi Sparkling Rosé Wine

70 cl ℮ BOTTLED BY CANTINE DEL DUCA S. CESARIO · NONANTOLA 7.8% vol.

Lambrusco It seems there is no end to the variations that can be played on the theme of this frothy Italian medium-sweet potion.
Tesco Lambrusco Rosé★ £1.79.

Listel The name of a vast vineyard right down on the sandy coastline of Mediterranean France in the Midi region. The pink wine is very light and quite dry.
Listel Gris de Gris★ £2.99, Thresher.

Masson California's most famous producer includes a rosé among his ubiquitous carafes. It is rather sweet.
Paul Masson Californian Carafe Rosé★ £2.89 Peter Dominic/£2.99 Thresher.

Mateus The Portuguese brand of pink that is essentially a variation on the *vinho verde* slightly sparkling theme – and which must have introduced more of us to wine than any other. Not beloved of wine buffs, Mateus is nevertheless a respectable-enough concoction, though by no means cheap for what it is. Few retailers stock it under £3.
Mateus Rosé★ £2.99, Littlewoods.

Navarra   Spanish region neighbouring – and rivalling – Rioja. An unusual, dry pink.
Sainsbury's Navarra Rosé★ £2.09.

Portugal   Not all Portuguese rosé is Mateus, but these two do taste like it, in other words slightly sweet and slightly sparkling.
Sainsbury's Portuguese Rosé★ £1.98.
Tesco Portuguese Rosé★ £1.95.

Provence   Some of the better rosés come from the south of France; these ones are quite dry.
Château de Beaulieu, Côtes de Provence Rosé★★ £2.95,
Waitrose.
Sainsbury's Rosé de Provence★★ £2.59.

Tavel   The name on the most fashionable of French rosés, made in the southern Rhône valley. Usually expensive – and better drunk young rather than when it has turned a strange orange colour after a couple of years.

Tavel Rosé, Malbec★★ £2.91, Willoughbys.

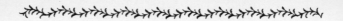

Red Wines Under £3

In spite of the fact that little more than a third of the wine we drink in Britain is red, there is a far wider and more interesting choice of it than there is of white wine. This is largely because red wine drinkers tend to be more picky – more adventurous, even – than those for whom wine is understood to be merely a pale, not-too-dry-not-too-sweet potion that has neither too much alcohol nor too many calories, and tastes marginally better than beer.

This latter group is, of course, by far the biggest part of the wine market, swallowing millions of bottles of Liebfraumilch and Laski Riesling – and so enabling the gleeful wine trade to stock up on less-fast-moving lines for customers who incline to something a bit more out of the ordinary.

The red wine listings here are consequently more extensive than those for white.

Aix en Provence Town north of Marseille in the French Riviera that is becoming as famous for its wine as for its chic tourist attractions. The reds are ripely delicious, though a little pricey for what they are.

Château de Fonscolombe, Coteaux d'Aix en Provence★★ £2.99, Adnams.

Marquis de Saporta, Coteaux d'Aix en Provence★★ £2.85, Bibendum.

Marquis de Saporta

COTEAUX
D'AIX-EN-PROVENCE

APPELLATION
COTEAUX D'AIX-EN-PROVENCE
CONTRÔLÉE

Mis en bouteille au Château

PRODUCT OF FRANCE

75cl ℮

Société Civile Agricole Fonscolombe, viticulteur
Marquis de Saporta, administrateur - 13610 Le Puy-Ste-Réparade

Algeria   Once the source of many an eye-watering beverage, but no longer. One interesting – and cheerfully rough – conversation piece.
Coteaux de Tlemcen 'Red Infuriator' ★ £2.39, Peter Dominic.

Algeria

French colonists, thirsty for the *vin ordinaire* of home, planted a million acres of vineyards in this torrid North African outpost during a century of occupation. Since it all ended with independence in 1962, Algerian wine has gently declined in both quality and quantity – helped along the downward slope by Islamic laws which somewhat dampen the enthusiasm of the local market for alcoholic beverages.

So Algeria is no longer the fount of cheap wines that once it was. But the few bottles that do still appear here are of reasonable value, and make something of a conversation piece, particularly among seasoned tipplers who nostalgically recall the heyday of Algerian plonk in the 1950s and 1960s.

Anjou   District of the Loire valley in mid-west France. Ordinary wines, light in body and dry in style, are sold as simple Anjou.
Sainsbury's Anjou Rouge ★ £2.25.
Tesco Anjou Rouge ★ £2.25.

Apollo   Typically silly name for a Greek wine, but don't be put off, for this is a fresh and full-flavoured red of real quality.
Apollo ★★ £2.09, Waitrose.

Ardèche French region just to the north-west of Côtes du Rhône country, and source of some good everyday reds, many from the Syrah grape which makes purply, slurpable young wines.
Sainsbury's Vin de Pays de l'Ardèche★★ £1.89.
Syrah Vin de Pays de l'Ardèche★ £2.45, Roberts and Cooper.

Arruda Portuguese red from vineyards near Lisbon; very rich and mature-tasting – highly recommended, and an extraordinary price.
Sainsbury's Arruda★★★★ £1.98.

Aude A *département* of south-west France encompassing several famous wine-growing districts, including Corbières, Fitou and Minervois (see separate entries). The ordinary wines or *vins de pays* of the *département* may lack the reputation of its better-known component regions, but they represent very good value as firmly fruity dry reds at bargain prices.

Asda Vin de Pays de l'Aude★ £1.65.

Littlewoods Vin de Pays de l'Aude★ £1.69.

Merlot Vin de Pays de l'Aude, Producteurs Réunis★★ £1.99, The Market, round and fruity, made from the Merlot grape of Bordeaux fame (*see* Merlot).

Merlot Vin de Pays de l'Aude, Vignerons Uccoar★ £2.52, Dolamore.

Sainsbury's Vin de Pays de l'Aude Carafe★★ £1.98.

Tesco Vin de Pays de l'Aude★ £1.89.

Vin de Pays Haute Vallée de l'Aude Cabernet Sauvignon 1985★ £1.89, Majestic, made from another renowned Bordeaux grape (*see* Cabernet Sauvignon).

Argentina

Prior to the hostilities of 1982, Argentina was sending us oceans of good-quality basic wines at prices that were almost ridiculously low. Admittedly, this had more to do with that benighted country's perpetually devaluing currency than it did with the efficiency of its winemakers.

Once familiar names – such as Franchette, which was selling at not much over £1.50 five years ago – are now shunned by a patriotic British wine trade with a long and selective memory. The very few Argentinian wines that do occasionally surface here are, it must be said, pretty dismal anyway – so it may not be entirely the Falklands Factor that is to blame.

Bairrada   Mid-western Portuguese province producing remarkable, richly fruity, smooth red wines – true *vinho maduro* ('mature wine') at some very low prices. To get the best from this wine, open the bottle several hours in advance and decant it; if you do not have a decanter, simply pour the wine into another, thoroughly clean, wine bottle. 'Airing' the wine in this way makes it taste even better.

Bairrada 1984 Imperio★★ £2.25, Peter Dominic.

Bairrada 1982★★ £2.69, Thresher.

Bairrada 1982/3★★ £2.25, Waitrose.

Bairrada 1982 Mealhada★★ £2.39 Peter Dominic/ £2.49 Gough Brothers.

Tesco Bairrada 1982★★★ £2.25, velvety wine reminiscent of fine Bordeaux red, and at a low price.

Banda Azul   Brand-name of a popular Spanish wine (*see* Rioja).

Barbera   Not a Latin hairdresser, but a black grape variety that flourishes in the Piedmont region of north-east Italy. It makes strong, long-lived, dark reds, particularly in the district around the southern Piedmont town of Alba.

Safeway Barbera d'Alba Fontanafredda 1984★★ £2.76, full, slightly prickly – ignore suggestion on label that you should open it hours in advance of drinking.
Sainsbury's Barbera d'Alba★★ £2.39.

Bardolino   A very light, dry Italian red made from grapes grown along the edge of Lake Garda in the north-eastern province of Veneto. Not serious wine, and not too headache-stimulating either.
Bardolino Cesari 1985★ £2.15, Majestic.

Bardolino Classico Lamberti★★ £2.69, Peter Dominic, good fruity flavour.
Bardolino Tardelli★ £2.15, Peter Dominic.
Bardolino Gianni & Domenico★ £2.69, Davisons.
Safeway Bardolino 1986★ £2.09.
Sainsbury's Bardolino Classico★★ £2.09, good value.
Tesco Bardolino★★ £2.09.

BARDOLINO
DENOMINAZIONE DI ORIGINE CONTROLLATA

SOFT LIGHT RED WINE

PRODUCE OF ITALY   SELECTED FOR TESCO

70 cle   VINO IMBOTTIGLIATO NELLA ZONA DI PRODUZIONE
TRAVE VERONA ITALIA   11.5% vol

Beaujolais Presumably the world's best-known red wine, this is the light, juicy, thirst-slaking product of the Gamay grape variety grown in the picturesque hilly district of Beaujolais around Mâcon in east-central France. Posh Beaujolais is expensive, and the cheaper stuff is at its best in the form of good 'Beaujolais nouveau', which floods on to the market each year only a few weeks after the grapes have been picked. Any nouveau wine priced over £3 is likely to be a waste of money, so stick to the cheaper ones – particularly from the wine-wise supermarkets such as Sainsbury's, Tesco and Waitrose.

Ordinary Beaujolais, which may be of indeterminate age, tends to be less enticing than the nouveau variety, and is not all that cheap. The 'Villages' wines are even more expensive, but in fact are better worth the money as they do at least have the scented and succulent flavour that makes good Beaujolais so sought after.

Beaujolais Marcel Baron★ £2.99, Peter Dominic.
Beaujolais Pierre Chaumont★ £2.59, Co-op.
Beaujolais AC★ £2.75, Noble Grape.
Sainsbury's Beaujolais★ £2.79.
Tesco Beaujolais★ £2.29.

Bergerac District of the Dordogne south-east of Bordeaux in south-west France; light red wines at good prices.
Asda Bergerac Rouge★ £2.09.
Bergerac Comte de Virecourt 1986★ £2.39, Oddbins, bit rough but flavoursome.
Tesco Bergerac Rouge★ £2.09.

Bodegas Las Orcas Decent Spanish wine with full, dry flavour.
Bodegas Las Orcas★ £1.99, Oddbins.

Bordeaux The very capital of the world's fine-wine business. Most of the wine from this maritime region of south-west France is expensive, and the ordinary, cheaper wines made from grapes grown beyond the

Bordeaux

This is the region that produces more top-quality red wine than any other in the world. Occupying the nondescript area of land around the river Gironde and its tributaries the Dordogne and Garonne in south-west France, the region was once known as Aquitaine and was, from 1152 to 1453, an English possession. This is supposed to explain why the British love red Bordeaux wine – known here as 'claret' – above all others.

Good claret is wonderful – and ruinously expensive. Even 'fifth-class' château-bottled red wine of the region costs £10-plus. The top wines, such as Château Margaux and Mouton Rothschild, can cost £50 and more per bottle.

Cheap claret is another story altogether. Because most red Bordeaux is made with grapes that have leathery skins and not that much flesh (namely the **Cabernet Sauvignon** variety), the wine needs time to mellow – that is, to pass through that curious process in which the bitter, mouth-puckering substances imparted by the skins and pips recede and the lovely fruitiness and richness of the wine emerge. And when claret is cheap, you can bet it is not old enough to have enjoyed the luxury of this vital passage of time before it reaches the off-licence shelf.

hallowed vineyards of the châteaux are anonymous and of questionable value when compared to their less-hyped rivals from Italy, Spain and Portugal. Everyday red Bordeaux is generally marketed in Britain as 'Claret' – the traditional English name for the region's *vin rouge*, humble or otherwise. *See* Claret.

Bouches du Rhône Scholars of French will know immediately that this means 'mouths of the Rhône'. It describes the basic plonk made in the delta formed by the Rhône river and the Mediterranean in France's warm south. The wines are lightweight.

Asda Vin de Pays des Bouches du Rhône★ £1.65.

St Michael Vin de Pays des Bouches du Rhône★★★ £2.15, Marks & Spencer, light but mature-tasting and

scented; exceptional value.

Tesco Vin de Pays des Bouches du Rhône★ £1.89.

Vin de Pays des Bouches du Rhône★ £2.19, Peter Dominic.

Bulgaria   Really excelling itself as a producer of good-quality and filthy-cheap wines; the production must be subsidized by the state to keep the prices so low. Most of the wine is sold on a 'varietal' basis – under the name of the grape that goes into it. *See* Cabernet Sauvignon, Mavrud and Merlot. The wine also appears under the Bulgarian own-label, Mehana (see separate entry). The bottom-of-the-range wine is very good and very cheap and appears under own-labels.

Majestic Bulgarian Red★★ £1.69.

Waitrose Bulgarian Red★★ £1.79.

Bull's Blood   Hungarian branded red wine of little distinction which hardly lives up to the butch reputation nourished by its advertising – based on the myth that ferocious Magyars drank the stuff to sustain themselves during the siege by Turks of the fortress town of Eger in the sixteenth century. The poltroonish Ottomans, so we are told, thought the red liquid being imbibed must be the blood of bulls, and fled the scene in a blue funk. Dutch courage doesn't win out, though, because the Turks came back a couple of years later and slaughtered the entire population of Eger. That part of the tale at least is true; it's tempting to believe the rest of it is, well . . . so much bull.

The wine is sold under its Hungarian name, *Egri Bikavér*, as well as under the translation, Bull's Blood of Eger.

Bull's Blood★ £2.99 Gough Brothers/Oddbins/Peter Dominic/Victoria Wine.

Bulgaria

Bulgaria is a prime source of excellent, cheap wine. In this most sternly socialist of Soviet satellites, the whole wine industry is state-controlled – and subsidized to keep prices competitive enough to attract plenty of imperialist gold from Western markets. All the wine is exported through the state monopoly, Vinimpex, and quality is consistently high.

The very basic wines are sold simply as **Bulgarian Red** and **Bulgarian White**, and the rest under their 'varietal' names – in other words the variety of grape that constitutes the wine. Bulgarian wines therefore appear in the listings under the following headings: reds – **Cabernet Sauvignon**, **Mavrud** and **Merlot**; whites – **Chardonnay**, **Pinot Chardonnay**, **Riesling** and **Sauvignon**.

The Bulgars are artful winemakers. Their expanding range of products is carefully tailored to Western tastes and indeed successfully imitates French styles in many respects – and at a much lower price. Bulgarian Riesling competes seriously with its German and Yugoslav counterparts of Liebfraumilch and Lutomer Laski respectively. For price and quality, it wins hands down.

Burgundy

The celebrated red and white wines of France's most chic vineyards are outrageously expensive. Famous-name burgundies such as Corton, Puligny-Montrachet and Volnay cost anywhere between £15 and £50 – twice or three times their prices of only a couple of years ago.

None of this, of course, need concern cheap-wine buffs. Except, unfortunately, that the prices of top burgundies have dragged those for everyday ones up into the stratosphere as well. Burgundy's basic white plonk, for example, Bourgogne Aligoté, is now extinct in sub-£3 price lists. Bog-standard Chablis, too, has shot up in price – way out of the £3 range. Even decent **Beaujolais**, the jolliest Burgundy *appellation*, is now rarely seen under £3.

It is a scandal, of course, and entirely brought about by the greed of the Burgundy *vignerons* who are cashing in on a current fashion for their produce in America – where, as we all know, they only like the best and don't give a goddam what they pay for it.

Until the bottom drops out of the burgundy market (if it ever does), the next best thing looks like the fast-improving *vin de pays* from further south. Look on the bright side: you can have a whole case of delicious Ardèche (Rhône Valley) red for the same price as J.R. and his Dallas cronies are paying – probably uncomprehendingly – for one bottle of boring old Domaine de la Romanée Conti.

Buzet Bordeaux backwater in south-west France, bordering Armagnac country (where the delicious brandy comes from); not much known here but one wine stands out.

Sainsbury's Buzet 1985★★★ £2.65, light in body but fine, dry distinctive flavour.

Cabernet Sauvignon This is the grape variety that wine bores drone droolingly on about above all others. Cabernet is the major ingredient in the ludicrously overpriced and overpraised wines of the Médoc – the most chic district of Bordeaux – such as Château Lafite, costing £70 a bottle from a vintage that won't be 'ready for drinking' for another twenty-five years or £200 a bottle for a vintage such as 1953 or 1961 which might just be potable by next Christmas.

The good news is that the Cabernet Sauvignon grows in many places other than the fairyland that is the Médoc. The vine does very well elsewhere in France, in America and Australia, in Italy and Spain, and in Bulgaria, for example. In these places it makes wine that, like many Bordeaux reds, needs a bit of time to 'mellow' but soon becomes delicious – and at a much lower cost, though not as often under £3 as would be ideal.

The cheap wines do not compare with the extravagant Médocs for quality, but good basic Cabernets should have an enjoyable mix of firm, deep fruitiness and dryness plus a complex, cleanly fruity smell. Colour will be purply when young, tending to brownish-red with a bit of age. Standards are inevitably variable, but it's worth looking for a good one.

Barossa Valley Estate Shiraz/Cabernet 1984★★ £2.69, Oddbins, an Australian blend with another famed French grape, the Shiraz (known in France as Syrah).

Bulgarian Cabernet Sauvignon 1982★★★ £1.95 Oddbins/Sainsbury's/£1.99 Gough Brothers/Majestic/ Peter Dominic/Roberts and Cooper/Tesco/Waitrose/ £2.09 Thresher/£2.15 Victoria Wine/£2.19 Davisons/ £2.35 Willoughbys.

Cabernet Sauvignon del Trentino 1978★★★ 75cl £2.59, Tesco, deep and delicious.

Cabernet Sauvignon Oriahovitza 1978★★★ £2.59 Majestic/Oddbins, Bulgarian 'Reserve', stacks of fruit, mature-tasting, classy.

Cabernet Sauvignon Vin de Pays D'Oc★ £1.95, Oddbins, from the south of France.

Franzia Californian Cabernet Sauvignon★★ £2.79,

Victoria Wine, plummy, good depth, needs to be open a while before drinking.

Hungarian Cabernet★★ £1.89, Oddbins, very cheap.

Murray River Cabernet Sauvignon/Shiraz★★ £2.59, Peter Dominic, similar blend to Barossa Valley version above.

Safeway Cabernet Sauvignon 1979 Hungarian Vintage Selection★★ £2.79, full and mature, a bit headachey!

Sainsbury's Australian Cabernet Shiraz★ £2.35.

Tesco Israeli Cabernet Sauvignon★ 75cl £2.19.

Cahors South-western French region with a name for making dark and impressively alcoholic red wines, from the Malbec grape. At the cheaper end, Cahors wines are lighter, but fully fruity and slightly exotic.

Tesco Cahors★★ £2.39.

California   Commercial American red wine seems to concentrate on being 'mellow' in character – so cut-price Californians are all soft and a little bland – but none the less drinkable for that.

Asda California Red★ £2.35.

California Red, Geoffrey Roberts★ £2.55, Peter Dominic.

Majestic California Red★ £2.55.

Paul Masson California Carafe★ £2.59 Oddbins/£2.89 Peter Dominic/£2.82 Willoughbys.

Sainsbury's Californian Carafe★ £2.35.

Campo Nuevo   Particularly delicious and good-value *tinto* (red) wine from Navarra in Spain, and very reasonable price.

Campo Nuevo Navarra★★★ £2.19, Victoria Wine, deeply coloured, richly scented and flavoured dry wine.

Cante-Cigale   Producer in Hérault in south-west France making a good and potent dry red from Cinsaut and Syrah grapes.

Cante-Cigale Cinsaut-Syrah Vin de Pays 1984/5★★ £2.25, Waitrose.

Castillo de Liria   Basic but decent dry Spanish red.
Castillo de Liria★ £1.89, Tanners.

Catalanes, Côtes   Wines from the hillsides in the Catalan region leading into the Pyrenees, on the French side. The wines have a good reputation for deep colour and flavour – and an even better reputation for being cheap.

Tesco Côtes Catalanes★ £1.89.

Victoria Wine Vin de Pays Catalan★ £1.99.

Caves Velhas   Big-time Portuguese wine firm. *See* Dão.

PRODUCE OF ITALY

CHIANTI

DENOMINAZIONE DI ORIGINE CONTROLLATA E GARANTITA

Full bodied dry red wine

SELECTED FOR TESCO

IMBOT TIGLIATO DALLA CASA VINICOLA
LUIGI CECCHIE FIGLI s.r.l
53011 CASTELLINA CHIANTI ITALIA

70 cl e

R.1.2/SI

Chianti The lively and distinctive red wine of Tuscany in central Italy, from the elegantly cultivated landscape between the historic cities of Florence to the north and Sienna to the south.

Chianti first made its name here through its unmistakable straw *fiasco* bottle, but these are rarely seen

CASTALDO

CHIANTI

DENOMINAZIONE DI ORIGINE CONTROLLATA

IMBOTTIGLIATO DA CA.VI.C. s.n.c.
GREVE ᴵⁿ CHIANTI ~ ITALIA

0,750 LITRI   R.1. 1367 / FI   11,5 % VOL.

now. Among the upmarket wines, the Chianti Classico
consortium figures largely – this is an association whose
members have estates on the better land at the region's
heart and have even higher standards of production than
are called for by the *denominazione di origine controllata* regulations. Classico wines carry the *Gallo Nero*

(Black Cock) symbol on their neck labels.

Chianti Carissa★★ £2.39, Co-op.

Chianti Cesari 1985★★ £2.19, Majestic, juicy and flavoursome, good price.

Chianti Classico Rocca Delle Macie★★ £2.65, Alex Findlater.

Chianti Putto 1985★★ £2.79, Davisons.

Littlewoods Chianti★★ £2.09, good value.

Safeway Chianti 1986★ £2.09, very light and pale-coloured.

Sainsbury's Chianti Classico★★ £2.45.

Tesco Chianti★★ £2.35, zesty flavour.

Tesco Chianti Classico★ £2.59.

Thresher Chianti★ £2.59.

Waitrose Chianti 1984/5★ £2.25, light and lively.

Choix du Roy   Decent French *vin de table*, dry and full-flavoured in an authentic refillable-type litre bottle; thoroughly evocative of *le bistro*.

Choix du Roy Vin Rouge★ litre £2.39 (£1.67 per 70cl), Tanners.

Claret   The red wine of Bordeaux. The best claret is wonderful, and expensive; the worst claret, however, is not all that cheap. This does not prevent virtually every wine retailer offering one or even several relatively cheap bottles of the stuff. Most low-cost bottles are of young wine – purple in colour and very often astringent in taste, though this is occasionally relieved by some flavour of fruit.

The wines below are some of those which have been enjoyable in the last year or so but, as with certain other wines, the vintage or even type of wine may have changed since the time of writing – even though the label will have stayed the same.

Asda Claret★★★ £2.25.
Duc de Rachelle Claret 1985★ £2.49, Oddbins.
House Claret, Peter Sichel★ £2.55, Majestic.
Jules Lenaire Claret★ £2.79, Roberts and Cooper.
Littlewoods Claret★ £2.59.
Tesco Claret★★ £2.29, cheap, but very drinkable, if 'unclaretlike'.
Victoria Wine Claret★ £2.69.
Waitrose Claret★★ £2.45.

Parting shot: 'claret' in many retailers' own-label bottles (including some supermarket chains who should know better) can be downright filthy – artificial-looking inky colour and mouth-puckeringly astringent texture are common faults. If you are not a seasoned red wine shopper, it might be wise to stay with safer – and cheaper – reds from other parts of the world. Don't make the mistake of thinking that because you have heard of claret that means it must be good!

Cooks New Zealand winery producing good basic dry red – a conversation piece at a reasonable price.
Cooks New Zealand Dry Red★ £2.99 Thresher/£2.59 Waitrose.

Corbières At the heart of the Midi in southern France, Corbières produces gutsy red wines at very good prices. Many of the wines come from individual estates and have their own distinctive characteristics – discovering your own preference is a pleasurable and affordable process.
Asda Corbières★ £1.99.
Château Ardolou Corbières★ £2.69, Thresher.
Château de Capendu 1983★★★ £2.19, Littlewoods, mellow and mature with good depth of flavour.

1984

Château
La Tour de Fabrezan

11,5 % vol

70 cl.

CORBIERES

APPELLATION CORBIERES CONTROLÉE

MIS EN BOUTEILLE AU CHATEAU

G.F.A. BOUFFET-CIBEINS
FABREZAN 11200 LEZIGNAN-CORBIERES FRANCE

Château de Montrabech Corbières★★ 75cl £2.58, Lay &
Wheeler.
Château d'Olivery Corbières★ £2.38, Willoughbys.
Château La Tour de Fabrezan Corbières 1985★★★
£2.15, Majestic.
Château Vaugelas Corbières★★ £2.39 Majestic/£2.55
Roberts and Cooper.

Corbières Marcel Brown★ £2.19, Peter Dominic.
Corbières Sica Foncalieu★ £1.89, Littlewoods.
Corbières Vignerons de Resplandy 1985★★ £2.45, Alex
Findlater.
Sainsbury's Corbières★★ £2.09.
Tesco Corbières★★ £2.09.

Cordier   Rather grand French wine firm which owns
fashionable properties such as Château Talbot in France,
but also makes some very good everyday wines under its
own name, including this robust and very flavoursome
dry red.
Cordier Vin de Table★★★ litre £2.49 (£1.74 per 70cl),
Gateway.

Corsica   Lying due south of Piedmont in Italy, the rugged island makes some very fine and rather alcoholic red wines, many with Italian-sounding names. Still a shade unfashionable (Corsican wines were until recently nearly all very rough plonks used for blending), they are very keenly priced.
Domaine de Fontanella★★ £1.95, Waitrose.
Sainsbury's Corsican Red★ £1.95.

Corsica

The island of Napoleon's birth and home of the vendetta is now gathering additional reputations as a warm and welcoming holiday resort and the source of some very drinkable wines. A French *département*, Corsica has its own designation under the *appellation contrôlée* regulations, and wines denoted *vin de Corse* are of guaranteed quality.

Costevin   French *vin de table* with a marvellously firm, fruity taste – best if decanted (simply into another, clean wine bottle will do) an hour or so before drinking.
Costevin★★ 75cl £2.64, Lay & Wheeler.

Côtes, Coteaux   Vast numbers of red wines from France bear the prefix *côtes* or the synonym *coteaux* to their names. It means, as explained in the White Wine section, that the grapes were grown on slopes – allegedly the best place to grow grapes, and therefore making better wine. Red Côtes and Coteaux wines are listed under their regions: *see* Aix en Provence, Ardèche, Catalanes, Duras, Gascogne, Lubéron, Lyonnais, Provence, Rhône, Roussillon, St Mont, Tricastin, Ventoux and Vivarais.

PRODUCE OF FRANCE

COSTEVIN

VIN DE TABLE FRANÇAIS

Mis en bouteilles par :

ED. COSTE & FILS. - 33210 LANGON

11,5 % vol

Sodal Langon

750 ml

Culemborg South African brand-name on a fruity, low-cost dry red made from a local grape, the Pinotage – a hybrid of Pinot and Hermitage grapes.
Culemborg Pinotage 1985/6★ £2.15, Waitrose.

Cuvée d'Adrien Very decent dry but softly fruity French *vin de table*.
Cuvée d'Adrien★★ £2.06, Lay & Wheeler.

PRODUCE OF FRANCE
VIN DE TABLE
Cuvée d'Adrien
70 cl   DRY WHITE FRENCH WINE   11,5 % VOL.
MARQUE DÉPOSÉE
MIS EN BOUTEILLE ET DISTRIBUÉ PAR S.B.V. · 78270 BONNIÈRES
Adrien Bertillon

Cuvée des Minimes Self-effacingly named but consistently good, dry *vin de table*.
Cuvée des Minimes★ £2.49, Peter Dominic.

Dão From this scrubby hill region of central Portugal comes the solid dry red *vinho maduro* that retails at such startlingly low prices in view of the age of some of the bottles on offer. These include the only ten-year-old wines to be found at under £3 anywhere, and the slightly younger ones are excellent value too.

Read the labels carefully when you are looking for bargains: as a basic guide, the older the wine the better, and if you find the word *garrafeira*, don't hesitate, as this broadly means 'top quality' in Portuguese wine parlance; *tinto* merely means red.

Dão Cardeal 1981★★ £2.39, Majestic, the motor trade's favourite.

Dão Caves Velhas 1979★★ £2.59 Gough Brothers/Peter Dominic/£2.69 Oddbins.

Dão Dom Ferraz 1980★★ £2.59 Peter Dominic/£2.69 Thresher/£2.99 Victoria Wine/£2.25 Waitrose.

Dão Imperio 1978 Garrafeira★★★ £2.99, Peter Dominic.

Dão Terras Altas 1982★★ £2.75, Alex Findlater.

Dão Vinicola Ribalonga★★ £2.69, Peter Dominic.

Sainsbury's Dão 1980★★★ £2.35, very good value.

Tesco Dão★★ £2.19.

Demestica Ubiquitous Greek-restaurant dry wine; not perhaps as cheap as it ought to be.

Demestica★ £2.49 Peter Dominic/£2.74 Willoughbys.

Domaines Is simply French for 'estate' or 'land', giving an additional but meaningless flourish to the winemaker's name on the label. *See* Lentheric and Minervois (for Domaine Maris).

Dom Ferraz Best-known of the Dão wine-producers in Portugal. *See* Dão.

Don Cortez Popular Spanish brand-name for a range of fair-quality wines at reasonable prices.
Don Cortez Red★ £2.19, Victoria Wine, softly fruity.

Don Mendo Strange brand-name for a full-bodied red from Cariñena near Saragossa in north-east Spain.
Don Mendo Especial Red★ £2.50, Sherston Wine Co.

Duras, Côtes de South-west French region not much heard of here – but this is a very good dry red.
Côtes de Duras Seigneuret 1985★★ £2.35, Waitrose.

Seigneuret®

DURAS

1984

70 cl ℮
11,5% vol.

VUE DE LA TOUR DE L'HORLOGE

Côtes de Duras

APPELLATION COTES DE DURAS CONTROLÉE

UNION PRODUCTION DIFFUSION
LANDERROUAT (Gironde)
PRODUCE OF FRANCE

MIS EN BOUTEILLES PAR LES PRODUCTEURS RÉUNIS

España, Vino de Once the name on an ocean of eye-watering plonk, but in these more grandiloquent times few bottles are so humbly labelled. There is one very well-priced and drinkable exception.
Sainsbury's Vino de España Tinto★ £1.75.

Faugères   Red from the Midi in France.
Faugères 1984★★ £2.59, Victoria Wine, firm flavour.

Fitou   An upmarket area within the Corbières region (*see also* Corbières). Dark, intensely flavoured dry reds that somehow have a flavour of the torrid south – if you use your imagination! Usually rather stylishly labelled, but don't let this put you off – Fitou wines are good anyway.
Fitou Cuvée Mme Claude Parmentier★★★ £2.75 Alex Findlater/£2.65 Gateway/£2.59 Peter Dominic/£2.99 Thresher/£2.79 Victoria Wine/£2.68 Willoughbys.
Fitou Le Carla★★ £2.59, Sainsbury's.
Fitou Rocflamboyant 1982★ £2.49, Peter Dominic.
Fitou Sarl Bouffet 1985★★ £2.29, Majestic.

Fonscolombe, Château de   *See* Aix en Provence.

French vin de table   Few bog-standard French wines are unpretentious enough to be labelled simply French Red, but one or two honest ones remain.
St Michael French Full Red★★ litre £3.50 (£2.45 per 70cl), Marks & Spencer, not all that cheap, but very good.

Victoria Wine French Full Red★★★ £1.99, fine colour, deep flavour.

PRODUCE OF FRANCE

FITOU

APPELLATION FITOU CONTRÔLÉE

1984

12% Vol. 70 cl

Mis en bouteille à F 11290-1168
par SARL BOUFFET, Camplong 11200 Lézignan

Gaillac   Yet another south-western French region producing decent, softish dry reds at good prices.
Domaine de la Valière 1985 Gaillac★ £2.15, Waitrose.
Labastide de Levis Gaillac Rouge★ £2.59, Peter Dominic.

Gard   Region to the west of the southern Rhône valley in the south of France. The better reds supposedly come from the Costières du Gard. The best wines have a roundness of flavour made more interesting by a very slight spiciness – a trait of many Rhône reds.
Asda Vin de Pays du Gard★ £1.89.

Château de Nages, Costières du Gard 1984★★ £2.19, Waitrose.
Domaine du Planas Vin de Pays de Gard 1984★★ £2.55, Alex Findlater.
Domaine St André La Côte, Costières du Gard★ £2.19, Davisons.

Greece

Now that Greece is catching on as such a popular holiday destination, and an EEC one at that, its wine producers are striving to cash in on the consequent rise in the popularity of Greek food and drink here in Britain.

Trouble is, Greek wines are not by any means as sunny and refreshing as a couple of weeks in Corfu undoubtedly is. Both the red and white wines available at under £3 here tend to be rather tired and dull in flavour – though there are honourable exceptions.

For those who enjoy the antiseptic aroma and resinous flavour of **Retsina**, there are a few brands on offer at under £3.

Gascogne   Gascony, as the British used to call it, was for a long time a little bit of England in south-west France, and the term was used loosely to describe our entire area of occupation in that region until we were booted out 500 years ago. Today, Côtes de Gascogne is merely the term for the *vins de pays* of the Gers district south of Bordeaux. The wines are very good value.
Asda Vin de Pays des Côtes de Gascogne★★ £1.99.

Hérault   Wine-lake-filling region of southern France producing some good if slightly rough reds – one or two are exceptional value. This tricky-to-pronounce name sounds in French conveniently like 'Aero', as in chocolate bar. *See also* Cante-Cigale.

Domaine de St Macaire Vin de Pays de l'Hérault★★★ £1.99, Waitrose, very dark colour with a dense, potent flavour, best with strong-tasting food.

Domaine St Germain Vin de Pays Co-op Louvinière★★ £2.53, Lay & Wheeler.

Tesco Vin de Pays de l'Hérault★ £1.69, a bargain.

Vin de Pays de l'Hérault Rouge★ £1.79, Majestic, cheap.

113

Israel   *See* Cabernet Sauvignon.

Jardin de la France   Picturesque name for *vins de pays* from the Loire.
Gamay Jardin de France, Rémy Pannier 1985★★ £1.99, Majestic, Gamay is the Beaujolais grape and this wine has a faint Beaujolais scent – very pleasant.

Jean d'Armes   The name sounds like a leg-pull, but this French *vin de table* is drinkable – and extremely cheap.
Jean d'Armes Rouge★ £1.69, Majestic.

Jumilla   Region south of Valencia on Spain's Mediterranean coast, lying inland from the 'Costa Brava' – so British holidaymakers may be familiar with the name as the local vino that washed down all that paella. The wine is dark in colour, firm, dry and rather exotic in flavour – and very good value for money.

Castillo Los Molinos Jumilla 1983★ £1.99, Davisons.
Jumilla Campolargo★ £1.99, Peter Dominic.
Sainsbury's Jumilla 1981★★ £2.15.
Tesco Jumilla★★★★ litre carton £2.09 (£1.46 per 70cl),
not just fruity and deliciously gluggable, but the
cheapest wine listed in this book.

Campolargo

ELABORADO Y EMBOTELLADO POR

BODEGAS FERNANDEZ, S.A.

ALC. 13 % VOL.
R.E. 5602-MU

PRODUCE OF SPAIN

70 cl e
R.S.I. 30.802-MU

JUMILLA
DENOMINACION DE ORIGEN

Saint Marcus

FULL BODIED RED WINE

SERVE AT
ROOM
TEMPERATURE

Produce of Spain   70 cl e

DENOMINACION DE ORIGEN LA MANCHA

Vino Tinto

SHIPPED AND BOTTLED BY CASSON LTD., BAYTREE LANE, MIDDLETON M24 2EJ.

La Mancha Vastly productive region of central Spain, and home to many of that country's worst wines. Those below are above average.

Asda La Mancha★ £1.69.

Gran Verdad★ £1.99, Willoughbys.

Saint Marcus Full Bodied Red★ £1.79, Co-op.

Lambrusco This peculiar, alcoholic version of lemonade comes from Italy's northern region of Emilia-Romagna, where they've been swigging the stuff for as long as anyone can remember. But the semi-fizzy, pale-red wine drunk in the beautiful towns – such as Bologna – of the locality is much drier than the sweetened version sold in Britain. More's the pity.

Lambrusco is a naturally sparkling wine, not a carbonated one. The bubbles are the product of a non-alcoholic fermentation which produces carbon dioxide; as this fermentation takes place with the wine trapped in an enclosed space, the CO_2 integrates with the wine to form bubbles. But don't expect it to be as fizzy as champagne – in fact, the bubbles subside almost as soon as Lambrusco is poured.

One more thing not to expect of Lambrusco: that it won't render you legless! To qualify for the DOC quality

mark, the wine must have at least 10.5 degrees of alcohol; a bottle of that and you're well on your way.

All the wines listed are of the same, semi-sweet type.
Asda Lambrusco★ £1.85.
Lambrusco Caricchioli★ £1.95, Oddbins.
Lambrusco Carissa★ £1.89, Co-op.
Lambrusco del Colle★ £2.39, Davisons.
Lambrusco Grasparossa di Castelvetro★ £2.35 Peter Dominic/£2.15 Sainsbury's/Waitrose.
Lambrusco San Prospero★ £1.99, Majestic.
Lambrusco Sansovino★ £2.29, Victoria Wine.
Lambrusco Tadiello★ £1.99, Tanners.
Lambrusco Zonin★ £2.15, Roberts and Cooper.
Littlewoods Lambrusco★ £1.99.
St Michael Lambrusco★ £2.25, Marks & Spencer.
Tesco Lambrusco★ £1.79.
Tesco Lambrusco di Sorbara★ £2.19.
Thresher Lambrusco★ £2.15.

Lello   Dry red from Portugal's Douro region.
Safeway Lello 1984 Reserva★★ 75 cl £2.59.

Lentheric   Southern French producer of a very firmly flavoured dry red made from two trendy grape varieties, Grenache and Merlot.
Domaines des Lentheric Grenache/Merlot 1983★★ £2.35, Majestic.

Lubéron, Côtes du   District east of Avignon in the southern reaches of the Rhône in Mediterranean France. Produces ripe and fruity lightweight reds, of good quality, and similar to Côtes du Rhône.
Côtes du Lubéron, Vignerons du Rhône★★ £2.55, Peter Dominic.

Lyonnais, Coteaux du   Around the ghastly industrial city of Lyons, just south of Beaujolais country, crafty French *vignerons* grow the Beaujolais grape (the Gamay) to make mock-Beaujolais that doesn't taste too unlike the real thing and costs a lot less.

Coteaux du Lyonnais Gamay 1986★★ £2.55, Waitrose.

Masson California's best-known winemaker and just about its only purveyor of cheap wines, for export purposes anyway.

Paul Masson Carafe Red★ £2.59 Gough Brothers/
Oddbins/£2.99 Thresher/£2.82 Willoughbys.

Mavrud   Black grape variety which prospers in Bulgaria and is reckoned to make that country's best red wine, particularly when grown in the southern province of Assenovgrad. The wine is deeply flavoured and dark in colour – and usually over £3.
Mavrud Assenovgrad★★★ £2.65, Peter Dominic.

Mehana   Brand-name for basic Bulgarian wines – which are also sold under retailers' own-labels (*see* Bulgaria).
Mehana Red★★ £1.79 Gough Brothers/£1.65 Oddbins/
£1.89 Peter Dominic.

Merlot   Grape variety that most distinguishes itself in Bordeaux, where it is the main ingredient in the world's most expensive wine, Château Pétrus (£200 a bottle for recent vintages is not unusual). For those of us on less lunatic budgets, the Merlot is available from other vineyards; it makes soft and fruity red wine well worth a couple of quid a bottle.

Bulgarian Merlot 1981★★ £2.09 Gough Brothers/£1.99 Majestic/£2.15 Oddbins/£1.99 Peter Dominic.
Safeway Hungarian Merlot★★ £1.85, dark colour, intense flavour, cheap.
Sainsbury's Merlot del Veneto★ litre carton £2.25 (£1.57 per 70cl), from north-east Italy and very cheap.
Yugoslav Milion Merlot 1984/5★ £2.05, Waitrose.

Minervois   An *appellation contrôlée* winemaking region of the Midi in south-west France where they make

really delicious red wines, concentrated in colour and flavour, superior to most of the plonk from the area, but not expensive. Domaine Maris is the best, but sadly not the cheapest Minervois.

Asda Minervois★★ £1.99.

Château de Gourgazaud★★★ 1.5 litres £5.75 (£2.68 per 70cl), Sainsbury's.

Château de Pouzols Minervois 1985★ £2.54, Willoughbys.

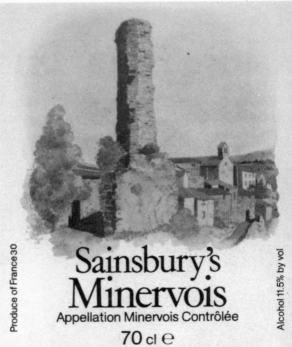

Produce of France 30

Sainsbury's
Minervois
Appellation Minervois Contrôlée

70 cl ℮

Bottled in France for J Sainsbury plc Stamford Street London SE1 9LL
by Celliers Jean D'Alibert, 11160 Rieux-Minervois

Alcohol 11.5% by vol

Domaine de Sainte Eulalie Minervois 1986★ £2.89 Davisons/Thresher.

Domaine Maris 1983★★★★ £2.75, Majestic, smooth, rich, intensely and thrillingly fruity, extraordinary wine.

Minervois Selection Marcel Baron★ £2.19, Peter Dominic, a bit coarse.

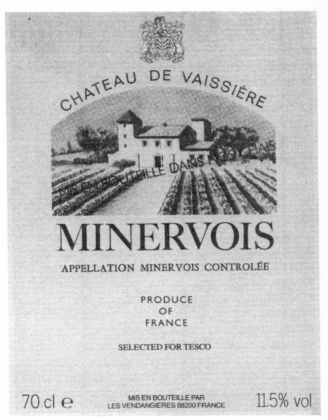

CHATEAU DE VAISSIÈRE

MIS EN BOUTEILLE DANS NOS CHAIS

MINERVOIS

APPELLATION MINERVOIS CONTROLÉE

PRODUCE
OF
FRANCE

SELECTED FOR TESCO

70 cl e   MIS EN BOUTEILLE PAR
LES VENDANGIERES 68200 FRANCE   11.5% vol

Minervois Sica Foncalieu ★ £1.89, Littlewoods.
Sainsbury's Minervois ★★★ £1.98, potent, dark and spicy, good value.
Tesco Minervois ★ £1.99.

Midi

The Midi is the broad coastal strip that runs from Montpelier on France's western Mediterranean shore down to the Spanish border. In these sunburnt climes grow the bumper crops of black grapes that make some of France's best cheap wines.

Corbières, **Fitou**, **Minervois**, **Côtes du Roussillon** – all are wines of the Midi, and are of a standard that was not dreamed of only a few years ago. New varieties of grape and improved standards in the vineyards and wineries have brought new life to this region, which remains the biggest of all French wine-producing areas, but now exports modest quantities of quality wine as well as pumping out oceans of *vin ordinaire* for domestic consumption.

All the good wines are red, full-flavoured and deeply coloured. They are usually pretty alcoholic, and some of the better ones – particularly Fitou – will improve if you keep them for a year or two before drinking.

Monsieur le Patron Very basic French *vin de table* that is good value dry red at the right price. Available only in magnum-size bottles.

Monsieur le Patron Rouge★ 1.5 litres £4.59 (£2.14 per 70cl) Peter Dominic/£4.79 (£2.23) Thresher/£4.15 (£1.94) Waitrose.

Montepulciano d'Abruzzo A mouthful of a name for a mouthful of a wine. Montepulciano is a black grape

MONTEPULCIANO
D'ABRUZZO
denominazione di origine controllata

BIANCHI

BOTTLED BY A.V.U.R. S.p.A.
OSIMO - ITALIA

PRODUCE OF ITALY

700 ml ℮   12%vol

grown in the Abruzzi, about halfway down Italy on the Adriatic side. The wine it makes is sunshine-warm and flavoursome – and even occasionally quite cheap.
Montepulciano d'Abruzzo★ £2.25, Peter Dominic.
Montepulciano d'Abruzzo Bianchi★★ £2.59 Majestic/ £2.84 Willoughbys.
Sainsbury's Montepulciano d'Abruzzo★ £2.35.

Murray River   *See* Cabernet Sauvignon.

Navarra   The great red hope from Spain – wines that match (well, nearly) the increasingly costly Riojas for quality, and substantially undercut them for price. Navarra lies between the Rioja region and the Pyrenees

Spain

Spain has space to spare. Its great land mass supports a population of only two-thirds that of Italy in an area twice the size. Consequently Spanish vineyards, which are dotted all over the country, are sprawling affairs yielding up great quantities of grapes at low cost.

Red wines from renowned regions such as **Rioja** and its neighbour **Navarra** are aged in oak barrels for two, three or more years before bottling, so they are fully mature when they go on sale; and yet prices remain very keen for these richly delicious wines. There are fresh white dry wines from these regions too, also at low cost.

The largest wine-growing region is the central Spanish province of **La Mancha**. Quality is mixed, but prices are commensurately attractive. In the undiscovered hinterland of the holiday coastline around Alicante and Benidorm, the **Jumilla** region is producing firmly fruity red wines that are now appearing in Britain at bargain prices.

Farther north in Catalonia, great winemakers such as the Torres firm in Penedes make an exciting range of red and white wines from an amazing variety of different grapes. The Torres basic dry white wine, Vina Sol, is a delight – though rather too close to the £3 mark these days.

Nationally, Spain has its equivalent to the French *appellation contrôlée* quality classification: the *denominacións de origen*, which guarantees that certain standards have been met – albeit less stringent ones than those applying in France.

in northern Spain. The wines are rich and smooth, and many have that distinctive 'vanilla' flavour that comes from being left for years in oak barrels (vanillin is a natural constituent of oak, in case you wondered).

Asda Navarra Red★★ £1.89.
Campo Nuevo Navarra★★ £2.19, Victoria Wine.
Gran Feudo Navarra★★ £2.15, Waitrose.
Safeway Gran Feudo Navarra★ £2.15.
Tesco Gran Feudo Navarra★★ £1.99.
Torrecilla Navarra★ £2.19, Peter Dominic.

NAVARRA

DENOMINACION DE ORIGEN
PRODUCE OF SPAIN

CAMPO-NUEVO

VINTAGE 1983

FIRM &
MEDIUM

46172

70cl e

SPECIALLY SELECTED AND BOTTLED FOR
THE VICTORIA WINE COMPANY, 31 BURY STREET, LONDON, S.W.1.

BY *Bodegas Cenalsa-Pamplona* / SPAIN

Embotellador R.G.S. N°30.99·NA·R.E.N°2921·NA-2·Exportador A-3112750-9

Nebbiolo The black grape that goes into all the smart wines made in Piedmont, the Italian province which borders with France. The wines are dense, alcoholic and all the better for a few years in the bottle to lose the harshness imparted to them by the Nebbiolo's thick skin. And this applies to the cheaper wines, too. At the very least, decant the wine (into another, clean wine bottle if necessary) several hours before drinking.
Tesco Nebbiolo del Piemonte★★ 75cl £2.69.

Oc   Not the Cockney term for Rhine wine (*see* Hock, John) but a large *vin de pays* region of western Mediterranean France extending from the Riviera to the Pyrenees. The strange name is derived from one of the *départements* it incorporates, Languedoc, which is so called because the local people say *oc* instead of *oui* (meaning yes, Jean).

In theory, the *vins de pays* of this huge area should be less good than its many trendier *appellation contrôlée* and *vin délimité de qualité supérieure* varieties, but in practice many simple Oc country wines are of great quality, as well as being commendably cheap. The catch is that few such wines find their way to this country. The two wines below are both made from the Syrah grape, and are silky, plummy and beautifully scented young dry reds.

Syrah Vin de Pays d'Oc★★★ £2.49, Oddbins.

Tesco Syrah Vin de Pays d'Oc★★★ £2.39, very good price.

Othello   Silly name for a perfectly decent dry red wine from Cyprus.
Othello★★ £2.69, Victoria Wine.

Othello
FULL BODIED RED
CYPRUS WINE

73 cl ℮

IMPORTED BY WOOLLEY, DUVAL & BEAUFOYS LTD. KINGSTON UPON THAMES.
PRODUCED & BOTTLED BY KEO LTD. LIMASSOL, CYPRUS.

Piat d'Or   Possibly the biggest-selling branded red wine in Britain. All that artful advertising ('J'adore le Piat d'Or', etc.) has to be paid for, so this very ordinary commercial red is by no means cheap.
Piat d'Or★ £2.59 Littlewoods/£2.69 Waitrose – but much more expensive elsewhere.

Pinotage   South African grape variety. *See* Culemborg.

Pinot Noir   The grape that goes into red Burgundy also makes expensive wine in other parts of the world. But there is one cheap one worth trying.

Hungarian Pinot Noir★ £1.89, Oddbins, potent and unusual.

Provence, Côtes de   Wines from the south of France are becoming trendy, and consequently expensive. Among the cheaper ones few are very interesting, but there is an exception.

Sainsbury's Côtes de Provence Rouge★★ £2.59, fresh and fruity, reminiscent of Beaujolais.

Quinta do Convento A Portuguese single-estate wine (*quinta* – pronounced 'keen-ta' – means 'estate'), this is a splendid *vinho maduro* (mature wine) of considerable age. Warm and full in flavour.
Quinta do Convento 1976★★ £2.49 Oddbins/£2.35 Peter Dominic.

Raboso del Veneto Raboso is the grape and Veneto the northern Italian region in which the vine flourishes. The result is a splendid garnet red, dry and firm wine. It always seems to taste better once the bottle has been opened for a glass or two, then re-corked and left for a few hours.
Sainsbury's Raboso del Veneto★★★ £1.85, extremely good value.

Rhône, Côtes du These ubiquitous wines come from the lesser vineyards of the southern Rhône valley in the

south of France. At the lower end of the price scale they seem much alike, often rather thin and sharp and not

Rhône

It is in the wide southern reaches of the river that the vines for the many and diverse **Côtes du Rhône** red wines flourish. Here the toothsome Syrah grape does well, and the potent Grenache too; they combine to produce wines which admittedly range from the poorest quality in great quantities to marvellous quality in very much smaller amounts.

Southern Rhône wines appear in all sorts of guises other than the simple Côtes du Rhône *appellation*. From east of the river come some excellent and low-cost *vins de pays* of the **Vaucluse** region, within which the two best-known *appellations* are **Coteaux du Tricastin** and **Côtes du Ventoux**. West of the river, the **Ardèche** region makes some marvellous wines from a wide variety of grapes. Southwards, there are the **Costières du Gard** and vast **Hérault** regions – both sources of a great volume of good everyday red and white wines. Right down on the Mediterranean beaches of the Camargue, trailing along in the sand, are the vines for the fresh and delicious **Listel** wines which are much enjoyed in local holiday resorts such as Sète – and which are now widely sold here as well.

always terribly good value. Of the wines listed, the best buys are probably the cheapest ones.

Asda Côtes du Rhône★ £2.39.

Château d'Aigueville Côtes du Rhône★ £2.79, Littlewoods.

Côtes du Rhône★ £2.59, Davisons.

Côtes du Rhône★ £2.69, Victoria Wine.

Côtes du Rhône, Barton & Guestier 1985★ £2.49, Oddbins.

Côtes du Rhône, Charles Prince 1985★ £2.70, Alex Findlater.

Côtes du Rhône, Rieu 1986★ £1.99, Majestic.

Côtes du Rhône Selection Marcel Baron★ £2.69, Peter Dominic.

Pierre Chaumont Côtes du Rhône★ £2.35, Co-op.

Safeway Côtes du Rhône 1986★ £2.29.

Sainsbury's Côtes du Rhône Villages★ £2.59, 'Villages' implies the wine comes from a more select group of vineyards.

St Michael Côtes du Rhône★ litre £3.50 (£2.45 per 70cl), Marks & Spencer.

Tesco Côtes du Rhône★ £2.39.

Thresher Côtes du Rhône★ £2.59.

Waitrose Côtes du Rhône 1985★ £2.45.

Rioja Northern Spain's famous wine district was pretty well unheard of until the prices of French wines went sky-high in the early 1970s and launched rich, oaky red Rioja as a thoroughly acceptable alternative to claret. Inevitably, prices for the best Riojas have crept up over the years, so that there are no really outstanding ones to be had under £3. Cheaper ones tend to be standard *tinto* (red) with little cask-ageing (*sin crianza*) or just a year or so of ageing (*vino de crianza*). *Reserva* wines have to have at least a year in cask and then

several years in bottle before they can be sold. Look on the bottles' back labels to see what style the wine is.

Asda Rioja ★ £2.45.
Rioja Anares Tinto Olarra 1984 ★★ £2.99, Oddbins.
Rioja Banda Azul Paternina ★★ £2.99, Victoria Wine.
Rioja El Coto 1985 ★ £2.79, Davisons.
Rioja Lancorta 1984 ★ £2.55, Waitrose.
Rioja Puerta Vieja Tinto 1983 ★★ £2.69, Majestic.
Rioja Vina Portil Tinto 1985 ★★ £2.49, Oddbins.
Rioja Vina Valduengo ★ £2.99, Co-op.
Sainsbury's Rioja Vina Alberdi 1983 ★ £2.95.
Tesco Rioja Vina Lanaga ★ £2.69.

Roodeberg South African wine made by the quaintly named Ko-operatieve Wijnbouwers Vereniging, known with merciful brevity as KWV. The wine is dark and potent and with a slightly 'stewed' taste that you either like or not!

KWV Roodeberg 1981★★ £2.99 Gough Brothers/Peter Dominic/Victoria Wine/£2.95 Thresher/£2.49 Waitrose.

South Africa

So far, sanctions seem not to have stemmed the steady flow of Cape wines into Britain. Like South Africa itself, the wines are mostly a bit of an acquired taste, but many are amazingly cheap in view of the great distance they must travel to reach us here in chilly northern Europe. Perhaps it is something to do with the cold the Rand has lately caught in the international money markets. See entries under **Culemborg** and **Roodeberg**.

Rosso Conero   A smooth Italian red wine.
Rosso Conero Villa Doro 1984★★ £2.49, Victoria Wine.

Roussillon, Côtes du   Roussillon is the part of the Midi in southern France which adjoins the Pyrenees, and is the source of many good, warming dark red wines, some with a 'hotness' of flavour that makes them distinctive, and delicious with food. The 'Villages' wines are best, but scarce.

Asda Côtes du Roussillon★ £2.09.

Côtes du Roussillon les Quatres Coteaux★★ £2.49, Peter Dominic.

Côtes du Roussillon Pierre Chaumont★ £2.09, Co-op.
Côtes du Roussillon Vignerons Audois★ £2.73, Dolamore.
Côtes du Roussillon Villages★★ £2.89, Roberts and Cooper.
Safeway Côtes du Roussillon 1986★ £2.49.
Sainsbury's Côtes du Roussillon★ £2.25.
Thresher Côtes du Roussillon Villages★★ £2.89.

St Chinian   Large *appellation contrôlée* district of the Hérault (see separate entry) making lightish and finely flavoured dry reds. Not much seen in Britain.
St Chinian★★ £2.15, Waitrose.

St Mont, Côtes de   From south of Bordeaux in southwest France, these are deeply coloured if slightly coarse wines – real picnic plonks.
Côtes de St Mont, Producteurs Plaimont★ £2.65 Adnams/£2.49 Lay & Wheeler.
Tesco Côtes de St Mont★ £2.15.

Sangiovese   The rather lyrical name of the grape that makes Chianti (see separate entry). It also makes wine in the province next door to Chianti's home of Tuscany, Romagna – and very good slurpable light red it is, too.
Sainsbury's Sangiovese di Romagna★★ 1.5 litres £3.75 (£1.75 per 70cl).

Sangria   A sort of winey fruit-punch base for making Benidorm's favourite party tipple. Mix it with lemonade or soda or even ginger ale – and add a belt of cheapo brandy for good luck. Don't drink it neat!
Real Sangria★ £2.99 Roberts and Cooper/Thresher/ £2.79 Victoria Wine.
Sainsbury's Sangria★ £1.75.
Tesco Sangria★ £1.69.

PRODUCE OF SPAIN

SANGRIA

SWEET REFRESHING DRINK
MADE FROM RED WINE
AND FRUIT JUICES

SELECTED
FOR
TESCO

SERVE CHILLED

70 cl ℮   SHIPPED AND FILLED FOR TESCO STORES LIMITED, CHESHUNT, HERTS
BY VICENTE GANDIA, VALENCIA, SPAIN   10% vol

Sanguinhal Splendid dry red wine from the Ribatejo region of Portugal, inland from Lisbon. Cheap but packed with flavour.
Sanguinhal Fonseca★★ £2.15, Peter Dominic.

Serradayres A fine dry Portuguese wine from the Ribatejo (*see also* Sanguinhal); mature-tasting, deeply flavoured – and very cheap for what it is.
Serradayres Imperio 1980★★★ £2.49, Peter Dominic.

Spanish Not so long ago, 'Spanish Burgundy', 'Spanish Sauternes' and the like were the very lifeblood of the plonk industry – and absolutely foul wines they were. Amazingly, some perfectly respectable retailers are still selling wines simply labelled Spanish this-or-that, and one of these bottles is a remarkable bargain.
Tesco Spanish Full Red★★ 1.5 litres £3.59 (£1.68 per 70cl), full-bodied and deep-flavoured.

Spanna   Memorable name for the Nebbiolo grape (see separate entry) as grown in the north of the Italian province of Piedmont, where it makes an intensely flavoured but fairly lightweight dry red.
Spanna del Piemonte, Agostino Brugo★★ £2.99 Oddbins/£2.95 Peter Dominic.

Syrah   Upmarket grape variety which goes into the finest wines of the Rhône in France, among many others. *See* Ardèche, Cante-Cigale and Oc.

Tonino   Brand-name for a respectable, slightly sweet red wine from Sicily. Reasonable value at the right price.
Tonino Vino Siciliano★ £1.99 Oddbins/£2.09 Thresher/ £2.54 Willoughbys.

Tricastin, Coteaux du   An *appellation contrôlée* district of the eastern Rhône Valley in the south of France where they make good, strong dry reds; they tend to be more concentrated in flavour and more likeable than run-of-the-mill cheap Côtes du Rhône wines. Often very good value.
Asda Coteaux du Tricastin★ £1.95.
Coteaux du Tricastin 1985★★ £2.19, Majestic.
Coteaux du Tricastin 1985★★ £2.25, Waitrose.
Safeway Coteaux du Tricastin 1986★ £2.15.
Sainsbury's Coteaux du Tricastin★★ £2.09.

Valdadige   Region of Italy's far north producing some delicious, featherweight reds.
Tesco Valdadige Rosso★★ £2.29, very light and slightly sweet.

Valencia   From the province surrounding the famous city on Spain's Mediterranean coast come some good ordinary reds (*see also* Jumilla).

Italy

The world's largest producer – and consumer – of wine is said to have some two million vineyards. The whole of Italy, from the northernmost regions of Alto Adige and Veneto to Sicily in the south, is well suited to the growing of grapes. So there is a huge and diverse range of Italian wines to choose from.

On a national scale, Italy regulates its wine through the quality-guarantee system under which the producers conform to laid-down standards. Qualifying wines carry the designation *Denominazione di Origine Controllata* (DOC). In view of recent wine-doctoring scandals, it makes sense for cheap-wine buffs to stick exclusively to *vino* that does carry this important guarantee.

And what a choice of cheap wine Italy has to offer! Curiously, the best buys are not the familiar **Bardolino**, **Frascati** and **Valpolicella** but the off-the-beaten-track wines that are now so cleverly sought out by the supermarket chains in search of good own-label bottles at rock-bottom prices. Tesco is the best source of these often brilliant bargains, and Sainsbury's is not far behind.

See the listings for, among many others, **Bianco di Custoza**, **Colli Albani**, **Raboso del Veneto** and **Verduzzo del Piave**.

Valmaduro Tinto★ £1.79, Majestic.
Vina Tinto, Rodrigo Perez★ £2.19, Peter Dominic.

Valmaduro *See* Valencia.

Valpolicella Italy's best-loved lightweight red plonk comes from near Verona in the northern province of Veneto. Delicate of flavour but with a distinctive shade of bitterness, it is genuinely at its best with the carbohydrate delights of pasta. The cheap ones are not greatly variable in quality, but those designated *classico* are

theoretically better, and those described as *superiore* are more alcoholically potent.

Asda Valpolicella★ £1.99.

Littlewoods Valpolicella★ £2.09.

Sainsbury's Valpolicella★ £2.09.

Tesco Valpolicella★ £1.99.

Thresher Valpolicella★ £2.39.

Victoria Wine Valpolicella★ £1.99.

Valpolicella Orsini★ £2.08, Noble Grape.

Valpolicella Carissa★ £1.99, Co-op.

Valpolicella Classico Lamberti★ £2.65, Peter Dominic.

Valpolicella Fabiano 1985★ £1.95, Oddbins.

Valpolicella Verona Antica 1985★ £1.99, Majestic.

Valpolicella Gianni & Domenico★ £2.49 Davisons/ £2.25 Roberts and Cooper.

Waitrose Valpolicella Classico★★ £1.99, substantial and smooth.

Vaucluse A big *vin de pays* area of the southern Rhône in the south of France, making none-too-serious dry reds that are largely indistinguishable from ordinary Côtes du Rhône.

Asda Vin de Pays du Vaucluse★ £1.85.

Tesco Vin de Pays du Vaucluse★ £1.89.

Vin de Pays du Vaucluse la Demoiselle★ litre £2.99 (£2.09 per 70cl), Peter Dominic.

Vin de Pays du Vaucluse, Pascal★ £2.25, Davisons.

Ventoux, Côtes du An *appellation contrôlée* subdivision of the Vaucluse (see previous entry), centred on the great Mont Ventoux. The wines are lighter in body but similar to other Côtes du Rhône, and at their best when still freshly young – so the newer the vintage year the better.

Asda Côtes du Ventoux★ £1.99.

Côtes du Ventoux Astier★ £2.39, Peter Dominic.
Côtes du Ventoux Delament Frères★ £2.85, Thresher.
Côtes du Ventoux Malbec★ £2.43, Willoughbys.
Sainsbury's Côtes du Ventoux★ £2.19.
Tesco Côtes du Ventoux★★ £2.09, young and fresh, delicious light wine.

Vino do Mesa   Simply means 'table wine' in Spanish. This is a reasonably full-flavoured and quite smooth dry red.
Safeway Vino do Mesa★ £1.75.

Vino rosso   Italy's answer to *vin rouge*, but not in quite such a plentiful supply – under the humble *vino rosso* label, anyway (lots of paint-stripping plonko italiano masquerades under much fancier names).
Tesco Vino Rosso★ £1.95.
Waitrose Carafe Red★ 2 litres £4.75 (£1.66 per 70cl).

143

Vin rouge   No shortage of this commodity, of course, but the better wine-wise supermarkets do offer perfectly drinkable *vin de table* under the name, and at very low prices. Bottle sizes vary from standard 70cl up to hefty 2 litre items.

Asda Vin de Table Rouge★ litre £2.29 (£1.60 per 70cl).
Sainsbury's Vin Rouge★ litre £2.45 (£1.72 per 70cl).
Tesco Vin Rouge★ litre carton £2.45 (£1.72 per 70cl).

Vin de Table Light Fruity Red Wine★ £1.89, Roberts and Cooper.

Waitrose Vin Rouge★ litre £2.39 (£1.67 per 70cl).

Vivarais An *appellation contrôlée* district of the Ardèche in the Rhône valley.

Vivarais★★ £1.99, Waitrose, soft, light wine.

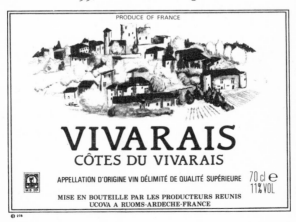

Wine in Boxes

Something like a sixth of the wine we drink at home in Britain is out of a tap. Bag-in-box plonk is therefore clearly here to stay. One good thing about the success of these handy containers has been that their big sales have brought their prices down to a more sensible level; five years ago, wines in boxes were very much more costly, litre for litre, than bottled equivalents.

Do bottled wines taste better, as the wine critics – particularly the Consumers' Association ones – have so loudly told us in the past? In one or two trial tastings in which I have participated, I have certainly noticed the differences between bottled and boxed versions, but just how significant these were I would be hard pressed to say.

Boxed wines are fine so long as you remember that only pretty basic stuff gets packaged in them. The producers claim that, once opened, the wine should be good for three months, but if you are the sort of wine drinker who takes that long to get through 3 litres, you would be a lot better off buying it in smaller quantities anyway. Apart from that, most wine does start to deteriorate long before three months is up.

For all that, there is no denying the convenience of boxes, and now that prices are more reasonable they can be a good buy. In the listings that follow, the prices in brackets show the equivalent price for the wine per 70cl – which helps make clear just how much, or how little, of a bargain the boxful in question is. All the boxes listed contain 3 litres, and all come out at less than £3 for 70cl.

White Boxed Wines

Australia
Australian Dry White★ £9.95, Willoughbys (£2.32).
Australian Medium White★ £9.95, Willoughbys (£2.32).
Berri Estate Dry White★★ £9.25, Peter Dominic (£2.16).

France
Colman's French White★ £7.65, Waitrose (£1.79).
Peter Dominic Vin de Pays du Jardin de la France★ £8.29 (£1.93).
Sainsbury's Gaillac Blanc★ £8.25 (£1.93).
Stowells Muscadet★ £11.45 Oddbins (£2.67)/£10.99 Peter Dominic (£2.57)/£11.69 Victoria Wine (£2.73)/£10.50 Waitrose (£2.45).
Stowells Vin du Pays de Tarn★ £8.99 Oddbins/Roberts and Cooper (£2.10)/£8.49 Thresher (£1.98)/£8.45 Waitrose (£1.97).
Victoria Wine French Dry White★ £8.49 (£1.98).
Waitrose French Dry White★ £7.15 (£1.67).

Germany
Colman's Liebfraumilch★ £8.95, Waitrose (£2.09).
Hock Deutscher Tafelwein★ £8.45, Waitrose (£1.97).
Mosel Deutscher Tafelwein★ £8.45, Waitrose (£1.97).
Silver Goblet Bereich Bernkastel★ £9.69, Peter Dominic (£2.26).
Silver Goblet Liebfraumilch★ £8.99, Peter Dominic (£2.10).
Stowells Liebfraumilch★ £11.19 Peter Dominic (£2.61)/£9.95 Sainsbury's (£2.32)/£10.99 Victoria Wine (£2.56).

Hungary
Sainsbury's Hungarian Olasz Riesling ★ £7.75 (£1.80).

Italy
Soave Amatti ★ £8.49, Peter Dominic (£1.98).
Tesco Soave ★ £8.39 (£1.96).
Thresher Soave ★ £8.25 (£1.93).
Waitrose Soave ★ £7.55 (£1.76).

Spain
Corrida Medium Dry White ★ £7.45, Thresher (£1.74).
Don Cortez Medium Dry White ★ £8.99, Victoria Wine (£2.10).

Yugoslavia
Cloberg Laski Riesling ★ £8.99, Peter Dominic (£2.10).
Lutomer Laski Riesling ★ £8.99, Peter Dominic (£2.10).
Tesco Yugoslav Laski Riesling ★ £7.29 (£1.70).
Thresher Yugoslav Laski Riesling ★ £7.99 (£1.86).
Yugoslav Laski Riesling ★ £8.99, Victoria Wine (£2.10).

Rosé Boxed Wines

Stowells Anjou Rosé ★ £10.49, Thresher (£2.45).
Tesco Rosé d'Anjou ★ £7.99 (£1.86).

Red Boxed Wines

Australia
Berri Estate Cabernet Sauvignon ★ £9.25, Peter Dominic (£2.16).

France

Colman's French Red★ £7.65, Waitrose (£1.79).
Safeway Côtes du Lubéron★ £7.99 (£1.86).
Stowells Claret★ £11.85 Oddbins (£2.77)/£11.69 Peter Dominic (£2.73)/£11.69 Victoria Wine (£2.73)/£10.50 Waitrose (£2.46).
Stowells Côtes du Rhône Villages★ £11.45 Oddbins (£2.67)/£11.49 Thresher (£2.68).
Stowells Vin de Pays du Gard★ £8.99, Oddbins (£2.10).

Italy

Valpolicella Amatti★ £8.49, Peter Dominic (£1.98).

Spain

Corrida Full Red★ £7.69, Thresher (£1.79).
Don Cortez Red★ £8.99, Victoria Wine (£2.10).

Sparkling Wines Under £4

First the bad news: champagne, on a budget of £4, is well out of reach. Even the cheapest supermarket own-label champagnes start at around £8 a bottle.

The good news is that there are alternatives. None is the same as champagne itself, but at half the price or less it would be too much to expect any convincing imitations.

There are three principal methods of making commercial sparkling wine. Grandest is the *méthode champenoise*, in which the newly made wine is bottled and then sealed, so that when a natural secondary fermentation in the wine occurs later, the carbon dioxide it produces cannot escape, so it integrates with the wine and *voilà* – bubbles. The process has to be accompanied by the tricky business of getting rid of the yeasty muck that forms in the bottle, but otherwise that's about all there is to it.

The *champenoise* process is a lengthy one, and labour-intensive (which to some extent explains the high price of the wine), so producers of cheaper sparklers generally adopt the second method. This is variously known as the Charmat technique, the *cuve close* or, in plainer words, the tank method. It sounds less glamorous than the champagne method, but differs from it only in that the new wine is put in a big, sealed tank, rather than in individual bottles, for the secondary fermentation.

The tank method is infinitely more respectable than the third technique – namely that of carbonating the wine by pumping air into it soda-syphon-wise. Carbonated wines stay fizzy for very little longer than it takes to pour them into the glass, so they are scarcely a great treat.

The small sample of sparklers that follows consists mostly of tank-method wines, except where the *méthode champenoise* (MC) has been used.

Asti   A city in the Piedmont province of north-west Italy where they produce more than 40 million bottles of sparkling wine a year – largely for the home market, as Italians drink more fizz than anyone else (barring only the British Upper Class, of course). They call the wine *spumante* ('foaming') and make it either in a medium-dry basic form or in a sweet version using Moscato grapes (*see also* Moscato).

Many Asti wines are expensive, especially those made by big-name Vermouth firms such as Cinzano and

Martini, but the humbler ones are perfectly good either as they come or as the bubbles for Bucks Fizz.

Asda Asti Spumante★ £2.99.
Asti Spumante Baldovino★ £3.61, Willoughbys.
Asti Spumante Sandro★★ £3.35, Waitrose.
Moscato d'Asti Gallo d'Oro★ £3.75, Waitrose, sweet.
Safeway Asti Spumante★ £3.49.
Sainsbury's Asti Spumante★ £3.39, sweet.
St Michael Asti Spumante★ £3.99, Marks & Spencer.
Tesco Asti Spumante★ 75cl £3.25.

PRODUCE OF FRANCE

G.F. CAVALIER

BLANC DE BLANCS

Vin Mousseux

BRUT ALCOHOL 10% BY VOL. 75cl

· CAVES DE WISSEMBOURG · WISSEMBOURG · FRANCE

Brut On a sparkling wine bottle, *brut* means 'very dry', and is a term applied to French fizzes as well as to champagne. There are a good number of different sparklers from France in the *brut* style, at somewhat varying prices. The eight below range from £2.59 to £3.99, with the cheapest probably the best of the lot.

Cavalier Blanc de Blancs Brut★★★ £2.79 Gough Brothers/£2.69 Majestic/£2.59 Oddbins, dry and clean, delicious *mousseux*.

Chanterelle Brut★ £2.99, Peter Dominic.
Chevalier Blanc de Blancs Brut★ £3.25, Davisons.
Duc de Grammoire Brut★ £3.45, Noble Grape.
Lafayette Brut★ £3.99, Thresher.
Paul Trudel Brut★ £2.85, Waitrose.
Pigalle Brut★ £2.99, Victoria Wine.
Veuve Valmante Brut★ £3.30, Willoughbys.

Cava The Spanish name for *méthode champenoise*. Cava wines are made in the Penedes region in the hills inland from Barcelona on the Mediterranean coast. The best are pretty expensive, but some decent dry ones are available under £4.
Sainsbury's Cava★ £3.85.
Tesco Cava★ £3.55.
Willoughbys Cava★ £3.66.

Demi-sec Applied to sparkling wine, this French term meaning 'half-dry' can safely be taken to mean pretty sweet — much sweeter, for example, than so-called 'medium-dry' wines such as Liebfraumilch. It's marginal, but *demi-sec* sparklers are not quite as sweet as those made from Moscato grapes (see next entry).
Chanterelle Demi-sec★ £2.99, Peter Dominic.
Duc de Grammoire Demi-sec★ £3.45, Noble Grape.
Lafayette Demi-sec★ £3.99, Thresher.
Paul Trudel Demi-sec★ £2.85, Waitrose.
Pigalle Demi-sec★ £2.99, Victoria Wine.
Veuve Valmante Demi-sec★ £3.30, Willoughbys.

Moscato The grape that goes into sweet sparkling wine from Italy, and also into a few French fizzes, where it has the name Muscat.
Asda Moscato Spumante★ £2.69.
Moscato Spumante Barbero★ £3.29, Victoria Wine.

Moscato Spumante Fratelli★ £2.75, Peter Dominic.
Moscato Spumante Italvini★ £3.25, Davisons.
Tesco Moscato Spumante★ £2.29.

Mousseux The French for 'sparkling', and a term used generically for a few decent fizzes from France. *Sainsbury's Vin Mousseux★★* £3.25, dry.

Rosé Pink sparklers are a rum lot, but the colour is pretty.

Cavalier Muscat Rosé★ £2.99, Majestic, medium-sweet.

Sainsbury's Rosé Spumante★ £2.69, medium-sweet.

Tesco Rosé Spumante★ 75cl £2.99, medium-sweet.

Veuve Chapelle Rosé★ £3.50, Noble Grape, dry.

SAINSBURY'S

Italian Sparkling Wine

Rosé
Spumante
MEDIUM SWEET

Alcohol 10% by volume

70cl ℮

Bottled in Italy for J Sainsbury plc Stamford Street London SE1 9LL
by I.V.I. Spa Canelli (Asti) Italy R.1 126 AT

Sekt It sounds as if it ought to mean dry, but in fact *Sekt* is German sparkling wine – and it may be any shade of dry or sweet. The term used for dry (well, fairly dry) German sparkling wine is, incidentally, *trocken*. It applies to all these.

Henkell Trocken★ £3.99, Peter Dominic.

Sainsbury's Sekt★ £2.95.

Peter Meyer Silver Cristel Sekt★ £2.95, Waitrose.

Splendid Deutscher Sekt★ £3.25, Davisons.

Waitrose Sekt★ £2.95.

Wehlener Abtei Riesling Trocken★ £3.42, Willoughbys.

Three

List of Retailers

The great majority of the wines included in Section Two are stocked by large retail chains, several of which have branches throughout the UK. Also included are a number of smaller wine merchants with a reasonable spread of branches. The few merchants mentioned who just have a couple of outlets do also run national mail-order operations. Write to or telephone them at the address or number given, and they will send catalogues and details of terms and delivery.

Adnams Wine Merchants
Upmarket East Anglian firm specializing in posh claret and the like, but also offering some good basic wines from around the world – though not at supermarket prices. Send for their amazing, glossy-magazine-size catalogue and mail-order details.
The Crown, High Street, Southwold, Suffolk IP18 6DP. 0502 724222.

Arriba Kettle & Co
Spanish specialists with a good mail-order list.
Buckle Street, Honeybourne, Evesham, Worcestershire WR11 5QB. 0386 833024.

Asda
One of the still-small number of supermarket chains

making a real effort to sell good wines cheaply (as opposed to bad wines cheaply, which anyone can do). Asda rather trades on its rock-bottom prices, so it is something of a mecca for cheap-wine seekers. There are about 100 branches around the country.

Augustus Barnett
Brewery-owned (Bass Charrington) chain that offers a few decent buys, but not half so many as it did when it was independently owned.

Bibendum
Trendy north London emporium with lots of smart wines and a sprinkling of bargains. Wholesale only – which means you must buy at least a dozen bottles, though these may be mixed. Price list and mail-order details (London deliveries are free) from the address below. Note that the wholesale-only status allows Bibendum long opening hours on Sundays: 11am to 6pm (and 10am to 8pm Monday to Saturday).
113 Regent's Park Road, Primrose Hill, London NW1 8UR. 01-586 9761.

Bottoms Up
Now that this eccentric chain has been taken over by the giant Grand Metropolitan group, it has been teamed with the conglomerate's main wine-merchant network, Peter Dominic. Bottoms Up shops will carry the same wines that appear in the listings under Peter Dominic – and a very good range they are.

Co-op
No chain matches the Co-op for sheer number of outlets – some 2,400 branches are licensed. The wines are not hugely exciting, but some are keenly priced. Note that not every Co-op sells every wine.

Davisons
Middle-sized chain with seventy-five branches in London and the home counties. They offer many exciting wines, though not all that many under the £3 mark. Note that they offer a good discount – 8.5 per cent – on purchases of twelve or more bottles of wine.

Dolamore
Long-established traditional wine merchant with a very interesting range, including some real bargains. They sell by mail order from their wholesale list.
Waterloo House, 228–32 Waterloo Station Approach, London SE1 7BE. 01-928 4851.

Alex Findlater & Co
London wine merchant with lots of good wines, and a few cheap ones. Mail order available.
77 Abbey Road, London NW8. 01-624 7311.

Gateway
Supermarket chain with a few bargains among the wines – but not always worth making a detour to find!

Gough Brothers
Moderately big chain (150 branches) offering many standard, branded wines, but rarely at prices that are not bettered elsewhere.

Lay & Wheeler
Essex wine merchant with a huge range of wines – their vast list has more than 1,000 different bottles. Although largely of the more expensive variety, the wines include some good cheapies. There is an efficient mail-order service.
6 Culver Street West, Colchester, Essex CO1 1JA. 0206 67261.

Littlewoods
High-street retail multiple with 100 branches all over the country. There is quite a reasonable choice of wines, many at very competitive prices.

Majestic
Far and away the leader in the 'wine warehouse' league, Majestic sell wines on a wholesale basis – minimum purchase a dozen bottles – from twenty outlets around the Midlands and southern England. Branches are open day-long, seven days a week. The range of wines is enormous: as many as 600, and prices compete even with the big supermarket chains. There is a nationwide mail-order service.
421 New King's Road, London SW6 4RN. 01-731 3131.

The Market
London chain of all-hours food shops which does a nice line in wines, including occasional real bargains. Prices are keener for the wines than they seem to be for the food.

Marks & Spencer
They more or less started the supermarket-wine boom, but now rather trail behind the leaders in terms of range and value. Still some good bargains, though.

Noble Grape
Wine warehouse firm with branches in London (Wapping), Surrey (Morden), Bristol and Cardiff. Minimum purchase a dozen bottles. Good range of wines, including many at very low prices. Rather random opening hours.

Oddbins
One of the best retailers of all. Oddbins have an im-

aginative stock at all price levels and somehow manage to employ particularly helpful and knowledgeable staff. Always very interesting shops to browse in. There is a mail-order service for those not living within reach of – or inclined to visit – their local branch (of which there are fifty around the country).

34–6 The Highway, London E1 9BG. 01-481 2944.

Peter Dominic

Britain's third-biggest high-street chain has 500 branches throughout the country. It has lately improved its wine stocks almost beyond recognition. Although owned by Grand Metropolitan (which also includes Watneys among the jewels in its crown), Dominics seems to have a free hand in its purchasing, so variety is rich – and prices very keen. Note that Bottoms Up shops are a twinned, jointly run chain, which will carry the same range.

Roberts and Cooper

Brewery-owned (Courage) retailer with 400 branches. Rather stronger on wines costing over £3 than under, but a few good bargains.

Safeway

Not a supermarket chain that distinguishes itself in the wine line, but it does have the odd good buy, and at some very low prices.

Sainsbury's

Britain's number one retailer of wine. One estimate is that one out of every six bottles of wine drunk in the home has been bought at Sainsbury's. The range is prodigious and the prices as low as can be found anywhere. There are 260 branches around the country.

Sherston Wine Co.

Wiltshire merchant with ten branches from London to Bath. Specializes in Spanish wines. Mail order available.

Sherston, Malmesbury, Wiltshire SN16 OLA. 0666 840644.

Tanners

Shropshire merchant with ten branches in Shrewsbury and surrounding areas. Extensive list of pricey wines, but a number of bargains too. Mail order available.

26 Wyle Cop, Shrewsbury, Shropshire SY1 1XD. 0743 52421.

Tesco

Neck-and-neck with Sainsbury's for choice, quality and value, Tesco's 330-odd licensed branches nationwide offer as many as 300 different wines. The choice of cheap wines is comprehensive, with even the smaller stores stocking 100-plus varieties – most of them under £3 and many under £2. The own-label wines that account for the great majority on offer are excellent value.

Thresher

The second-biggest high-street wine merchant, with 800 branches, Thresher is – naturally – brewery-owned (Whitbread). It offers mainly branded wines that are also available elsewhere, but does have a few bargains.

Victoria Wine

The largest of the high-street retailers, with about 900 outlets. Owned by a brewery (Allied this time), it carries many of the products made by fellow members of the Allied Lyons conglomerate – such as Grants of St James's, Harveys of Bristol and Showerings (of

Babycham fame). But there are bargains, too – particularly the 'Victoria Wine Selection' wines bearing the red symbol on their labels.

Waitrose
Smart supermarket chain that is part of the esteemed John Lewis Partnership. Eighty branches, but all in the Midlands and south. A marvellous selection of more than 200 wines – and at very good prices. Ranks with Sainsbury's and Tesco as a veritable paradise for cheap-wine hunters. It's only a pity there are no branches north of Birmingham.

Willoughbys
Manchester wine merchant with associated branches in Chester (George Dutton) and Liverpool (Thomas Baty). A big list which includes many low-cost wines, though not all are bargains. Mail-order service.
53 Cross Street, Manchester M2 4JP. 061-834 6850.

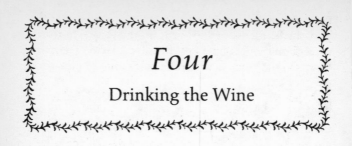

Four

Drinking the Wine

Keeping, Serving and Drinking Cheap Wine

The etiquette of serving and drinking wine remains to most of us one of the unsolved riddles of the universe. Screeds have been written by generations of social gurus on what wine to drink when and with what, which kind of glass to drink it out of, at what temperature and so on *ad nauseam*. It has all contributed to the ludicrous snobbery that attaches itself to the subject – putting off countless potential wine-gluggers in the process.

One of the fundamentally great things about cheap wines is that none of the almighty wine bores, past or present, would deign to suggest what the punter should do with them – bar pouring the lot down the sink, that is. Cheap wine, everyone acknowledges, tastes the same whether you drink it out of a paper cup, a billy can or Old Mother Riley's hobnail boot.

Cobblers, as they say, to that. Cheap wine is like any other: it tastes best out of a clean glass. I'll even go further and say that it tastes better out of a *big*, clean glass. Why? Because you will enjoy any wine better if you can give it a good sniff before taking a mouthful. So what you need is a glass large enough to hold a generous quantity with no need to fill it up to the brim. About the right size is one with enough room to take a quarter of a 70cl bottle, meniscus included; fill the glass two-thirds up and you've got a decent measure, leaving plenty of room to poke your nose in for a quick intake of the good old bouquet.

As to what *kind* of glass, that really is a matter of etiquette. Some of the experts say that plain, uncut, uncoloured glass is the only suitable variety because it allows the drinker an uninterrupted view of the wine's glorious colour. If your wine is of the under-£2 variety, you may well prefer not to contemplate its hue, of course, but maybe the experts have a point.

Another area in which the experts offer endless disputations is that of temperature. White wine should be chilled, we are told, and red wine should be *chambré*-d (served at room temperature, in polite Brit circles).

All true. But *how* cold and at *what* 'room' temperature? The trouble with such sweeping advice is that it has caused most white wine to be dished up at a temperature that freezes out the fillings in the teeth, and reds at the blood-warmth of a centrally heated room – which can make even the most expensive wines taste peculiar.

It is up to all of us to drink our wine just how cold or warm we like, but it is worth bearing in mind that whites that have had more than a few hours in the fridge will be stone-cold and that this will unquestionably mask the true flavour. Now that may be a good thing if the wine tastes vile anyway, but if you are mildly curious to know what your £2 or even £3 bottle tastes like, take it out of the fridge a half-hour or so before opening it.

As for red wine, it tastes all the better for being slightly cool, because when served up very warm it loses its refreshing quality. Most cheap wines are, inevitably, young ones still full of the fresh fruitiness of youth (provided you've got a decent cheap bottle, that is) and will not be enhanced by being warmed up.

One complication of red wine is the 'to breathe or not to breathe' question. Among the experts, there are several schools of thought as to whether corks should be pulled well in advance and whether the wine should be decanted. Some say 'breathing' improves all red wines. Others say it does nothing for any red wine. Who's right?

In the listings, I mentioned in the notes appending a few wines that they had tasted the better for being decanted. Other than these specific recommendations, I cannot say what the process would do for reds in general, but it does seem that decanting has no *harmful* effects even on the cheapest wines – provided that the decanter is not left unstoppered for hours on end so that the wine oxidizes and consequently turns flat and horrid, like the morning-after dregs.

What does nothing at all for red wine is the curious ritual of opening the bottle an hour or more before serving time. This merely exposes the few square centimetres of liquid on the surface, and certainly doesn't amount to letting the wine 'breathe'. Only the action of glugging the stuff into another container will fulfil that function.

How long can you expect an opened bottle to last before it starts to taste dreggy? In my own experience, even cheap wines stay quite fresh if re-corked and re-opened twenty-four or forty-eight hours later. White wines kept properly stoppered in the fridge can go on for several days. Red wines after the second opening do have a tendency to Brasso-flavour, so don't expect the *vino rosso* to taste too brilliant after more than two days.

And what of keeping wine that hasn't yet been opened? This is a trickier question altogether. One popular view is that all wine improves the longer it is kept. Not true. Basic *vin de pays* reds and their equivalents from other countries will generally decline in tastiness after only a few months. And virtually all low-cost whites are better the younger they are.

Some reds can be kept for a year or more and may improve: Portuguese Bairrada and Dão are examples; Cabernet Sauvignon from Bulgaria, Fitou from southwest France and Nebbiolo wines from Italy will 'mellow' with time into smoother, rounder condition. But don't overdo it – none of these sub-£3 wines are made as true *vins de garde* (keeping wines) of the château-bottled French variety which are intended to last ten, twenty or more years.

For simple economy, it does pay you to buy wine in reasonably large quantities. Most of the best bargains are from the supermarket chains or wine warehouses, and these are not the sort of places you're going to pop into every evening on the way home from work. By stocking up on a single trip, you save yourself running out of plonk and having to dash out to the corner off-licence where you are quite likely to end up paying a usurious price for some frightful brand-name bottle.

True, if you have a stock in the house you're more likely to say 'Let's have a bottle of wine'. And why not? It's as good an excuse as any.

Pubs, Wine Bars and Restaurants

Just like most high-street off-licences, most pubs are owned by breweries. And just as brewery-owned shops are filled with the proprietor-company's various products, so are the pubs. This is fine for beer drinkers – after all, you don't go into a Courage pub if you want to drink Watneys Beer.

If your preferred tipple is wine, however, it's another story. Brewery-owned pubs simply stock the wines that head office tells them to, and that means the wines which associated companies produce, regardless of their quality. And the sad fact is that nearly all these wines are boring brands which are at best uninteresting and at worst undrinkable.

The prices demanded make for little consolation. They vary wildly according to which brewery and what part of the country, but £1 for a glass of pub plonk is par for the course. What's more, you cannot predict what size of glass you will get for all that money. While the beer drinker is guaranteed the full imperial measure of pint or half-pint, the wine bibber is left guessing as to whether a glass's contents amount to anything like a reasonable slug. There have been various unsuccessful attempts in the past to cajole pubs into using a standard wine glass of 125ml (one-sixth of a 75cl bottle), but the crazy variations in sizes still prevail.

There is very little the pub customer can do about the lack of regulation, quality and value in wine, other than simply staying away or drinking something else. In fairness, though, there are a few pubs – particularly free houses unencumbered by brewery conglomerates with lousy wines to offload – which do offer decent wines in decent glassfuls.

Failing the availability of a wine-conscious free house, there is of course the option of the now widespread wine bars. In the good ones, you are in a different league. Naturally, the wines are better value by the bottle than by the glass, and you have the luxury of choosing from a range.

What's more, wine bars do not have the luxury of monopoly as enjoyed by the brewers, so they must keep their prices to a level which will attract wine drinkers – as opposed to pub-wine drinkers, who tend merely to be towed along in the wake of beer drinkers. There are plenty of wine bars offering 'house' bottles at around £4 and while that is doubtless a 100 per cent mark-up on what it cost from the wholesaler, it's still a bargain when compared to the £1 pub glass which probably contains about one-eighth of a bottleful.

Mark-ups in wine bars and restaurants are utterly arbitrary, but you can usually count on the price being double what you would pay retail. This is particularly true of cheaper wines. After all, it costs a bartender or waiter just as much in terms of labour to unpack, store away, find again, chill if necessary, open and pour a £2 bottle as it does a £20 one! Some good establishments put a very much lower premium on their posher wines than they do on cheap ones, in the hope of encouraging customers to try a special bottle – but no wine bar or restaurant does the same for the plonk-lover.

Choosing the right wine when confronted with a lengthy list is purely a personal matter of preference. The best-value wines may well be the 'house' ones as these must always be offered at a lower price than named bottles. Where house wines don't look too tempting, it can be a good idea to stick to the varieties which tend to make the best bargains in the shops:

Bulgarian red rather than 'claret', new-vintage *vin de pays* rather than overpriced Blue Nun, and so on.

Cheap wine when eating or drinking out should be regarded as a contradiction in terms, given that whatever wine you order, you will pay through the nose for it. But then the whole point of an outing is the sense of having a bit of a fling, so don't worry about it! Or if you must, make tracks for one of those diminishingly traceable emporia, the restaurant without a liquor licence, and take your cheap wine with you . . .

The Hangover

There is a wild rumour afoot that cheap wine produces a worse hangover than expensive wine.

This is, of course, absolute rot. It is the quantity of alcohol that determines the extent of the morning-after horrors. And most cheap wine contains exactly the same amount of alcohol as most expensive wine. The fallacy arises out of simple ignorance of the fact that the average hangover candidate is more likely to get a skinful of the cheap stuff than of the expensive stuff. Barring freeloaders and millionaires, that is.

So how much can you drink before the abdabs set in? Various medical reports appear to concur that the average man can drink about a bottle of wine a day without wrecking his liver – provided that's all the alcohol he consumes. For the average woman, the ration is half as much – owing to metabolic differences between the sexes, we are told.

These quantities apply only to matters of the liver, however, and for many people as much as a bottle – or a half – every day might be far too much from all sorts of other points of view. A bottle of wine, for example, contains around 500 calories, which may well be as much as a quarter of the ideal daily intake before the flab starts mounting up. (Slimmers should note that there's precious little difference between red and white wine calorie-wise.)

Meanwhile, back to the hangover. People of normal

weight can expect to metabolize a modest-sized glass of wine every hour. This means that if you stay four hours at a dinner party and have four glasses of wine, you won't get plastered and you shouldn't get a hangover (but don't assume you would pass the breathalyser – such matters are notoriously unpredictable).

It also helps if you're eating while you're slugging the wine and, believe it or not, you are less likely to suffer if you don't smoke.

But if, like most of us, you just can't restrain yourself on some special occasion from going right over the top, what can you do to cope with the potentially calamitous effects that lie in wait?

Prevention

There are lots of wonderfully crackpot prophylactic measures. One which I actually tried in the selfless endeavour of researching this book was the device of some long-dead naval officer who used to prepare himself for the rigours of wardroom cocktail parties by downing a sherry-glassful of olive oil. It certainly worked for me: the experience made me feel so sick I couldn't face a drink all evening.

As to methods that function in a more literal sense, there are certainly many subscribers to the Drinka Pinta Before You Start school. Milk is high in fat and this is helpful in coping metabolically with alcohol. What's more, the bulk of the liquid does something to lessen the capacity to drink anything at all.

Dehydration is a major feature of the best hangovers, producing such entertaining symptoms as the mouth like the proverbial Kookaburra's Khyber. So, a pint or two of water before, after or amidst the revelry has some merit. This would be another benefit of milk if that was the preferred beverage.

Cure

In the end, it's only the cures that count, of course, because you are unlikely to heed the risk you're taking. Being three sheets to the wind, after all, is a state in which the reveller is most disinclined to take precautions. So, when the hangover must be faced, what to do?

In my researches I have come across only one 'cure' that could cope with a Force 9 hangover, and that is to remain utterly inert for as long as possible. This calls for staying in bed all day if necessary, offering the most convincing excuses to anyone consequently inconvenienced as can be summoned up in the circumstances.

For a milder hangover – following, say, a couple of bottles of *vino collapso* the night before – here are my top five recommended remedies, in ascending order of efficacy.

Number Five Follow the persistent boozer's brave measure of gulping down a shot of Fernet Branca, the highly alcoholic herbal preparation that tastes like nothing else on earth. It may make you gag a bit, but it does have a remarkably soothing effect on the stomach – which mysteriously pervades the rest of your physiognomy. There is another potion which shares Fernet Branca's reputation, called Underberg, but I cannot personally vouch for its efficacy.

Number Four Drink several cups of Earl Grey tea, with milk but no sugar. I have no idea why this works so well, but it does wonders for several occasional sufferers of my acquaintance – notwithstanding the social *faux pas* of adding milk to this most aristocratic of beverages.

Number Three   Mix yourself – or, better, have some-one mix for you – a Cowshot: half a can of Campbell's consommé soup with an equal measure of water, warmed up to dissolve it thoroughly. Plus two dashes of Tabasco and a teaspoonful of sherry or cider vinegar. Stir it all up with a couple of ice cubes to make it palatably cool and glug it down.

Number Two   A bottle of cold beer. This does, of course, carry a health warning: more drink on the morning after is a step closer to the slippery slope of alcoholism. But the fact remains that in extreme emergency, once every blue moon, a cold beer can be effective.

Number One   This requires planning ahead. Find a chemist who stocks homeopathic preparations. Purchase some *Nux Vomica*. It should come in the form of little white pills which taste quite sweet – you simply crunch them and swallow. On the day of doom, take two pills every hour for six hours.

With a bit of luck, your faith in cheap wine – or whatever else it was – will be restored.

A selection of bestsellers from Sphere

FICTION

WANDERLUST	Danielle Steel	£3.50 □
LADY OF HAY	Barbara Erskine	£3.95 □
BIRTHRIGHT	Joseph Amiel	£3.50 □
THE SECRETS OF HARRY BRIGHT	Joseph Wambaugh	£2.95 □
CYCLOPS	Clive Cussler	£3.50 □

FILM AND TV TIE-IN

INTIMATE CONTACT	Jacqueline Osborne	£2.50 □
BEST OF BRITISH	Maurice Sellar	£8.95 □
SEX WITH PAULA YATES	Paula Yates	£2.95 □
RAW DEAL	Walter Wager	£2.50 □

NON-FICTION

AS TIME GOES BY: THE LIFE OF INGRID BERGMAN	Laurence Leamer	£3.95 □
BOTHAM	Don Mosey	£3.50 □
SOLDIERS	John Keegan & Richard Holmes	£5.95 □
URI GELLER'S FORTUNE SECRETS	Uri Geller	£2.50 □
A TASTE OF LIFE	Julie Stafford	£3.50 □

All Sphere books are available at your local bookshop or newsagent, or can be ordered direct from the publisher. Just tick the titles you want and fill in the form below.

Name _____

Address _____

_____

Write to Sphere Books, Cash Sales Department, P.O. Box 11, Falmouth, Cornwall TR10 9EN

Please enclose a cheque or postal order to the value of the cover price plus:

UK: 60p for the first book, 25p for the second book and 15p for each additional book ordered to a maximum charge of £1.90.

OVERSEAS & EIRE: £1.25 for the first book, 75p for the second book and 28p for each subsequent title ordered.

BFPO: 60p for the first book, 25p for the second book plus 15p per copy for the next 7 books, thereafter 9p per book.

Sphere Books reserve the right to show new retail prices on covers which may differ from those previously advertised in the text elsewhere, and to increase postal rates in accordance with the P.O.